The Risk Taker

The Risk Taker

John Paul Gutschlag

Cover design by Joe Morua

ISBN: 153319615X
ISBN 13: 9781533196156
Library of Congress Control Number: 2016907932
CreateSpace Independent Publishing Platform
North Charleston, South Carolina

Table of Contents

About the Author

—❧—

JOHN PAUL GUTSCHLAG HAS SERVED as a CEO for more than forty-five years, first as the founder of a software development company that he took public in 1968. This company, Affiliated Computer Systems Inc., was sold to Mercantile National Bank in Dallas, later taken public, and became ACS, traded on NYMEX. Next, he served as president and later chairman of the board of Keystone Life Insurance Company for fourteen years. Finally, he has been CEO of a national insurance agency and a third-party administrator for the past twenty-eight years.

His experience has afforded him seniority and a patriarchal position in the student-health-insurance industry. He knows and has connections with many of the largest insurance and reinsurance companies in the domestic United States, as well as with Lloyd's of London and other prominent companies in Europe. He's also developed relationships with hundreds of brokers and agents, along with business relations with many prestigious US colleges and universities.

Preface

⟍ᴓ⟋

THIS IS THE STORY OF my CEO experiences from 1983 to the present. Please don't panic, as quite a few are presented in summary. I start with a tragic event that only later in reading will you find the outcome. Actually, I begin with a little background on the health-insurance market for students and the various parties that make it possible for students to obtain insurance. The second chapter discusses with some detail the ostrich industry, and the reader may wonder what this has to do with health insurance. It doesn't and only shows that I branched out in my personal life—first in finding a ranch where I could chill and relax on weekends, but because of my business head, I found ways to use the property to make a buck. It actually exploded in potential. Suffice it to say the resources spent and my risk taking cost me in my prime business. I want the reader to understand this, as business diversions and my time spent seeking meaningful relationships for my personal life resulted in vulnerability as I grew my bread-and-butter business in the student-health market. I wasn't bouncing back and forth; I was trying to balance all at the same time. We all know the human brain doesn't function in this manner.

I describe deceptive trade practices that exist industrywide. I show examples of how the students are victimized and include a unique comparison to the Madoff fraud.

I personally paid a price for my risk taking that I describe in detail. I believe you'll find that experience interesting and insightful and with thought-provoking solutions.

I love the student-health-insurance industry, as it's like an old Western gold-mining town: devoid of most regulations and guidelines, somewhat lawless, and damn sure home to *High Noon* shootouts that seriously impact many a gunslinger's business reputation or income level. It's a market not for the faint of heart, as the risk taking involved is akin to what any high-stakes Las Vegas gambler would indulge in.

Through the combination of participating parties in the enterprise, there were strategies executed to overcharge student health premiums industrywide. Over the past decade, collaborating with thousands of schools and millions of victimized students, the enterprise billed students, their parents, and educational subsidies out of billions of premium dollars.

Some of the world's largest insurance companies garnered exorbitant profits. Also, the participating school officials, agents, brokers, and administrators shared in the scam.

Please note that, throughout the book, names and places have been changed to protect the innocent.

Opening

I EXITED HIGHWAY 276 TO enter the Bar GM Ranch—recognizable by a large sign hung sixteen feet overhead, enough room for an eighteen-wheeler to negotiate. I followed a winding, well-kept gravel road past a treed area to where the former homes of my mother and my daughter, Tracy Lynn, and her first husband had once stood. The two trailers are now gone; only manicured and cut lawns remained. I passed two tanks where, in years past, cattle drank and escaped the hot weather with belly-soaking baths. Those cattle were Simmental, a large breed from Switzerland.

I crossed a cattle guard at the top of the hill, and there was my ranch-style house looming in the distance. It was a nice spread, with lush landscaping and a pool. Evergreen trees lined the drive, and to the right and left of the drive were large pens, pipe fencing, and a pasture area where, only twenty months before, more than six hundred ostriches had been moving and shaking, running speeds of forty to forty-five miles per hour, alongside chick pens full of babies that were the cutest offspring on the planet and a feed silo that used to contain fifteen tons of special feed pellets formulated for ostriches.

I drove into a large five-space carport and shut down my GMC Sierra 2500 4x4 with custom interior, bumpers, and sound system, the dual pipes growling to a halt. I walked into the garage, through the back door, and into our back kitchen area. Barbara was waiting for me at a small kitchen table. This was a planned meeting where I was supposed to lay out the asset split that would end our thirty-eight-year marriage. We greeted each other amicably but without much emotion.

She then told me that she had just taken cyanide tablets that we had once used to kill coyotes for the protection of the ostriches.

CHAPTER 1

The Enterprise

As a CEO, I knew how to access the sum of the parts that made up the enterprise. Each school had its own means of access to the enterprise, and I knew how this worked from my many years of experience. Trying to market directly to a school when there was a strong broker involved usually gave you a quick exit, meaning there was no real chance to secure or write the business.

When access to a school account is through the broker, it usually exposes dual experience reporting, meaning the broker has more favorable experience (lower loss ratio) than the direct approach.[1] The broker explains this as more current experience, showing more premium and fewer paid claims than what the bid indicated. A bid or RFP (request for proposal) formally solicits the marketplace with specifications as defined by the school and how the response is to be submitted back to the school procurement office or designated person who handles bids. In any case, the broker is just setting him- or herself up for a higher commission (up to 15 percent) to access this "exclusive" experience or account control. In other cases, the school official would have more favorable reporting available to those he or she wanted to work with.

---

1 Experience equals claims divided by premium. Thus, a 75 percent loss ratio equals a claims fund of 75 cents for every premium dollar.

George Washington University had such a person, where if you did nice things for her—drinks and dinner, a gift to the health-care center, or, on occasion, repairs for her vehicle—then that special experience report was yours, as was the opportunity to provide a better (lower) premium rate. You see, this was all for the "benefit" of the students, who indirectly signed her paycheck. What was never addressed was the fact that maybe the students didn't need this self-serving fiduciary involvement and would have been better off if they were directly involved or had input on all the facts.

Deception is a major factor executed by the "fiduciary" involvement on a national scale. Each year several hundred million dollars in health premiums is overcharged to students based on agent/broker commissions, health-center fees, and unnecessary third-party fees.

Take the example of including a provider network access fee that is added on to the claims cost and a rebate paid directly to the broker by the network administrator. This inflates the claims cost by 8–10 percent while omitting the rebate savings. Thus, fraudulent reporting, illegal rebates to broker, and just another form of account control is being achieved.

Deception is the basis for fraud and is practiced by most schools with their connections to the enterprise. I'll provide much more detail on this subject in later chapters.

Take a minute to review the parties involved, as it will be more meaningful as you progress through the book. The student-health-insurance industry consists of the following parties that together or in some combination provide a product of accident-only or accident-and-health-insurance coverage to students throughout the United States. This is a multibillion-dollar niche market and subset of the gigantic national health-insurance market. The contract of insurance coverage (master policy) is with the school who represent the students enrolled.

There are various types of enrollment: mandatory; mandatory with waiver, if other coverage is proven; and voluntary.

1. **Insurance Companies:** These are large, financially secure companies, "A" rated by A.M. Best as either property and casualty or life chartered. Commonly referred to as *carriers*, they maintain proper licensing by the state and the financial backing needed to issue coverage, taking anywhere from 0 to 100 percent of the risk. Often, they subcontract with TPAs (third-party administrators) for marketing, premium collection, and claim services.

2. **Reinsurance Companies:** These companies enter into contracts with primary carriers to take some of the risk, usually under a quota-share contract.[2] In essence, they provide backup capital to the insurance companies. They are active in monitoring program performance, particularly if they take a larger portion of the risk (i.e., over 10 percent). They are domicile worldwide with huge amounts of investment capital.

3. **Third-Party Administrators (TPAs):** These entities are usually independently owned and operate as companies licensed by the state to collect premiums, pay claims, and perform other administrative functions under contract with insurance companies (carriers). This may include marketing the product as well.

4. **Brokers and Agents:** They are licensed by the state to sell product(s) directly to schools.[3] They have developed contact relations with school officials, who many times designate them as *brokers* or *agents of record*, which indicates that all outside communication is directed through them, giving them ultimate

---

2 Quota-share risk: a divided percentage of risk involving all participating parties (insurance companies and reinsurers).

3 School: a school district, college, or university.

control of the schools or accounts. Brokers and agents must be appointed by insurance companies to represent those carriers to the clients. An individual broker or agent is often appointed by several carriers.

5. **School Officials:** These are the primary school representatives involved with the student insurance (could be the chancellors, vice presidents of student affairs, superintendents, or health-center directors). They are focused on getting what is best for the students, who indirectly pay their salary and make their career paths possible. Many schools have insurance committees that functions as defusing entities for decisions, as no one person *wants* ultimate control over final decisions. The committee prolongs the officials' longevity.

CHAPTER 2

The Ostrich Industry

Figure 1. Adult male ostrich

I BOUGHT A TWO-HUNDRED-ACRE RANCH (called a *ranchette* in Texas) in 1983 as a getaway and dabbled with raising cattle on a small scale with approximately seventy-five to a hundred head. I started with Black Angus and Hereford bulls, and later I switched to Simmental. I liked the concept of large animals raised and sold by the pound without proportionate cost increases. Plus, they were beautiful brown-and-white animals. I planted, cut, and baled my own coastal hay, usually 180 six-foot-round bales per season. I always had plenty of natural tank water and could sell a six-month-old calf weighing seven hundred pounds for $600 plus. So, in a year, I was able to pay for the haying operation, vet bills, truck/farm equipment, gas/maintenance, and weekend food and beer/wine consumption.

In 1985, a new ranching animal began to appear in the warm climate areas in the United States: the ostrich. A member of the Ratite family, these flightless birds are "cousins" of emus and kiwis. The ostrich is a magnificent specimen. Adult males stand eight-and-a-half to nine feet tall and weigh 400 to 450 pounds. They can run forty-five miles per hour with great athleticism, bobbing left and right as they turn on their "afterburners."

From a business standpoint, every part of the bird had marketability: the known feathers for the fashion industry; hides for luxury leather products such as boots, belts, vests, coats, purses, and wallets; and the large toenail for exquisite jewelry. Even the eyes had value, since optometrists had been having success with corneal transplants (it seems the eye characteristics of the ostrich and humans are identical). The sleeper was the meat. Oh *wow*! You wouldn't believe it! It looked and tasted like your best beef steak ever and was low in cholesterol and fat and high in protein. It turns out that some of the best chefs in four-star restaurants would feature ostrich medallions on their daily entrée menus.

I visited several ranches that were just getting started and then joined the American Ostrich Association (AOA) and helped start a local chapter. It was a start-up venture, and I bought two pairs of breeders for $25,000. I named them Fred and Wilma and JR and Callie.

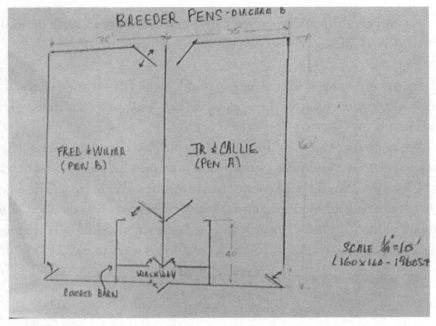

Figure 2. Diagram of 75-foot-by-150-foot breeding pens

We started construction on two breeding pens that I designed for easy off-loading, feeding, and veterinary access. These were later replicated to twenty pens, housing pairs and trios (one male and two hens) totaling twenty breeding males and thirty-two laying hens.

I always respected the math for a laying hen. She would cycle into the season usually March through October, and if the male was about his business, she would lay every other day like clockwork. Egg production per hen per year was 70 to 110 eggs.

Figure 3. Embryo-to-live-chick ratio

Egg Production: Example 100 eggs
* **Fertility**: 90 percent (male and female aren't always compatible)
* **Hatchability**: 90 percent (always some difficulty coming out of the egg)

- **Survivability**: 70 percent (high mortality rate in early period)
- **Live Chicks**: 55–60 percent (at three months)

In summary, a hundred eggs would yield fifty-five to sixty live chicks three months after the eggs were laid. This was considered great production.

We constructed a hatching and chick facility complete with A/C, a backup generator, and state-of-the art NatureForm incubators and hatchers. Chick pens would hold twenty-five little ones with heaters. The chick is hatched as a cold-blooded animal and changes to warm-blooded in its first three months; thus, warmth and environmental conditions are most important for survivability. Total cost of all this was around $150,000.

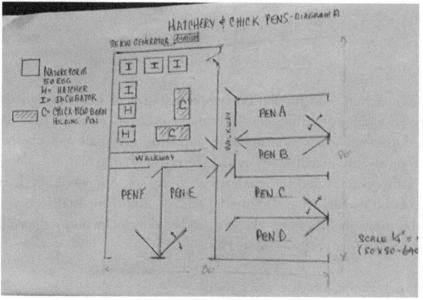

Figure 4. Hatchery and chick pen diagram

The breeder market was showing great potential for growth in 1991, with the industry expanding globally. Products were in demand, far surpassing supply. We were selling six-month-olds that were six feet tall and 135 pounds for up to $8,000 each.

This was still a breeder's market. Initially, I did my own trucking for people buying birds for breeding purposes. I had my own specially equipped trailer and trucked between eight and ten birds to locations like Lubbock, San Antonio, and several remote farms in Louisiana. All transactions were in cash. The buyer would look over the birds as I unloaded them and give me a wad of cash.

Later, as the processing cycle kicked in, where the birds were being sold for product, I trucked to a plant in Fort Worth that had converted from horse rendering to ostrich. Soon I only had to pay a couple hundred to their driver, who would pull up to the barn I had constructed for delivery and loading from the pasture. I could load twenty to twenty-five birds in a half hour, pay the driver $200 in cash, and receive a check in the mail for approximately $18,000 three days later.

I was contacted by two businessmen brothers from Okinawa, Japan. They had a profound interest in starting an ostrich facility on their home turf, including a processing plant. They visited me at my ranch and became intrigued about the future and what it might bring to their homeland. I made a deal with them that one could train at my facility for one month, and then we together would ship my birds to their facility, which the other brother was making ready.

The plan was to lease a Boeing 747 and crate fifteen nine-month-old birds, ten females and five males. We could sex gender at this age. They made the arrangement for a leased aircraft, one-way trip for $250,000, and the air company would construct the crates. We split the cost of the flight, and I was to receive $15,000 per bird. I was comfortable netting $100,000 and the promise if successful to be granted an exclusive for future shipments. Keep in mind the lease plane could fly cargo loaded back to the states for additional revenue. So, it seemed like a win-win for all.

Figure 5. Six-month-old ostriches

I decided to put together a limited partnership to sell units in this promising market. I formed an LLC and named it JBJ Ostriches LLC. I put together a private placement memorandum that didn't require SEC approval as long as the memberships didn't exceed thirty-five units. It was a first-class package, professionally exhibiting the ostrich market in four-color printing. The units were $10,000 each. The manager was the Bar GM Ranch, which would manage the breeding and raising of chicks for subsequent sale. The fee was 8 percent per year.

I was the CEO; Barbara, my wife, was president; and Jim Wilson was the marketing director. Wilson knew investment brokers who had clients interested in passive income. The commission was 9 percent. The package would include breeder birds, seven females and five males, purchased from the manager for $183,500. The five-year *pro forma* showed a total membership value at $1,223,281, with a distribution provision of 50 percent manager and 50 percent members. If this initial offering was successful, the package could be replicated infinitely. I had the land, know-how, and facilities to handle more than four hundred breeders, and this could be a "Texas cash cow" the likes not many have ever seen.

The American Ostrich Association (AOA) had been working on a national contract with Burger King, which would assure us a profitable total-end market. The high-end meat could more than hold its own, and leather products were in high demand. I had also partnered up with a processing plant in Pittsburg, Texas, just fifteen miles from my ranch. We passed USFDA inspection and approval.

The Achilles' heel in the industry was a lack of capital infrastructure and the fact that South Africa could compete with North America hands down. They would have a black woman sit in a chick pen all day for one dollar and calm the little buggers. (Chicks typically stress out over sudden sounds or environmental changes, resulting in a high mortality rate.) We couldn't compete with the lowering of prices, particularly on hides. South Africa literally froze us out, and farms started dropping out of the market, particularly those that had just gotten started on the end of the marketing chain. It wasn't a Ponzi scheme, as no one entity was making the profits based on early entry.

There was still a window to sell limited partnerships, as passive investors are the last to know what's going on in the trenches. However, even with my marketing guy guaranteeing a 100 percent package sale, I got cold feet. I could clearly see investors getting hurt or, at the very least, losing their investment. I had been on that side many times in the past—investing in limited partnerships for oil drilling, boxcars, low-income housing, and others—and always lost in the long run while the general manger made out handsomely. I guess, in the back of my mind, this is what gave me the idea in the first place. But again, the vibes weren't right, and I smelled lawsuit, lawyers, depositions, and courts of law.

The emu market hurt us. They came on after the ostrich as a cheaper (and easier to handle) way to raise chicks. Their problem: the emu was a bird a third the size of the ostrich that didn't have the feather or hide markets. Again, as with cattle, if you're going for meat production, why raise smaller animals? Ranchers who exited the market literally turned the birds out to roam the countryside as another member of the wild animal species.

I hung on until 1998, first selling the young birds and then my original breeders, some that had been worth $100,000 a pair just three years prior. My Okinawa deal got a little smelly as three birds died in flight, literally bashing themselves to death in the crates. Others were injured. These animals could not handle stress of any kind. My Japanese partners wanted me to split the cost of the birds, so I actually lost $12,500 on the risk venture. Also, I received word that other ranchers who had tied into the Asian expansion had bizarre happenings occur. One was an unsolved shooting that left one prominent AOA official dead in a corral.

The ship was sinking, and I literally rode her down to where my last four breeders were left with six little chicks at their sides, taking care of them as they would on the great African Serengeti. It was sad, but overall it was a great ride—an unforgettable risk-taking experience that satisfied my desire to work with animals but left me about $250,000 lighter in my wallet.

The real aftermath was the declining and ultimate failure of the business. It was the last link that my wife, Barbara, and I had between us. She was so good at hatching and raising the young chicks and spent untold hours doing so. Her life was the ostriches. My life was insurance/ostriches, or in reverse order for a while. My selfish desire to not get old together led to our divorce. She deserved better. By the hand of God, I've deserved and to date have received the worst. If I had to do it all over again without the benefit of current knowledge, it's hard to say that I wouldn't have repeated myself. I'm a risk taker, and there can be a price to pay for that. May God forgive some of my decisions and those I've hurt.

An Ostrich Story

The speed of this species is amazing. One day I was in a breeder pen to gather a newly laid egg, keeping my eyes on the male, who traditionally guards the nest or laying area. Typically, the hen lays on cycle, at the same time every other day and in the same place. I know not to take my eyes off the protector. On this particular day, I was in the pen and going to pick up the egg, and I noted he was 150 feet from me. Then, boom, he was on me! Do the math. The bird runs forty-five miles per hour, and that's out of blocks, so in less than two and a half seconds he was on me.

Years before, I had traveled to Texas A&M to visit with a renowned veterinarian, Dr. Kevin Winslow, and discuss his studies on ostrich. He actually had four birds (two pairs), and he was experimenting with them and observing their behavior. I asked him, "How would a person protect himself if one of the 'big boys' got to him or had him cornered?" He said to lie down, curl up into a fetal position, and shield your head with your arms.

Well, here we were, and this wasn't the lab. This bird was angry and perturbed that I was messing with his egg. My memory recalled Dr. Winslow's advice, and I went through the prescribed steps, but I couldn't help but wonder as I shook from fear on the ground in a fetal position, *What if he proceeds to just kick and stomp the life out of me*? It seemed like two days went by with that nine-foot, 450-pound male standing over me, looking for some movement. Any sign of fight or aggression and he was prepared to take me out. As my senses returned, I remembered that the ostrich has a Gestapo-style kick, so the trajectory would miss me lying on the ground. (He really didn't know how to stomp, either.)

As my trembling became less apparent, the ostrich got bored (short attention span) and walked away. With his backside to my eyes, I bailed out of the pen. Never again would I underestimate ostrich speed and quickness. From that point forward, two of us gathered eggs: one for decoy and one as a superfast retriever.

ANOTHER STORY: ROUND 'EM UP AND HEAD 'EM OUT

I was in the process of selling six-month-old birds. I was doing business with a slaughterhouse that had its own tractor-trailer rig and driver. This was great, as heretofore I had done it all myself. Anyway, my setup involved having the rig back up to my loading area. I previously had run about twenty birds into the barn, and my job was to run one bird at a time down the chute to where my son-in-law, Carlos, and his brother, Marcos, would guide the lone traveler into the trailer.

This was Marcos's first rodeo, and he was somewhat apprehensive. Anyway, I was in the barn with twenty fidgety, six-foot, 135-pound scrappers. I grabbed one by the neck six inches below the head and, in an athletic move, with the other hand, slipped a cutout sweatshirt sleeve over his head. The bird was bewildered, and I grabbed him by the wings, head on, with my chest to his, and moved him backward. This was easy to do, as the bird couldn't dig in, and I could guide him by pushing his wings. I got him to the chute, yanked off his head sleeve, and pushed him down the chute into the rig. I then yelled to Marcos, "Just be sure he makes it inside."

Well, this young scrapper completely ran over Marcos, knocking him down on his Keister, but the bird somehow still ended up inside the trailer. I said, "Marcos, you all right?" I then instructed, "Stand aside when they come down; just be sure they don't break to the side and get out. Hey, if you wanna quit, no big deal!"

Carlos had done the job before, and I didn't want anyone to get hurt. Marcos was a pretty good-size linebacker himself, so he spit, blew out both nostrils, and said, "Bring the next one."

Well, I had my role down pat and said, "Here he comes."

When an ostrich runs at you, it's deceiving, because it's not a straight line. He wavers left and right in a zigzag fashion. This bird hit Marcos head on, but this time Marcos was ready. He took the blow and then proceeded to chop block and karate chop the bird to the ground. Marcos then pushed him upright and straight into the trailer. I commented, "Damn, Marcos, just guide 'em. Don't go to war!"

Marcos replied, "Send another; I'm ready!"

CHAPTER 3

Operating Companies

THE UNDERWRITER

UNDERWRITERS ARE BEHIND-THE-SCENES IN RISK taking. They determine the degree of risk and establish a premium rate that *should* be equitable to the insuring company and consumer.

My father was a life insurance underwriter for forty-three years. Life insurance has a tremendous backup of statistics and mortality tables by occupation to aid the underwriter in determining a profitable, fair, and equitable premium rate. As an example, morticians, house painters, and bartenders are notorious alcoholics and therefore are rated up (premium increased) so much per thousand in life coverage. A whole-life policy taken out at age forty for a mortician may be $35 per $1,000 of coverage more than a normal occupation such as an office worker. Underwriters, in this sense, really are simply following established guidelines and have little influence on final rates to be released to sales departments. This is why my father disliked his job. It was boring, with no challenge and every day same as yesterday. I remember, when growing up, how I said to myself, "I don't want a job like Dad's."

In the sports-gaming industry, risk is established but literally covered by balancing the participants on both side of the wager. If the line on Super Bowl IXLX is three and a half points New England, the gaming personnel are sure to balance both sides of the risk (i.e., equal

New England bettors giving up three and a half points and equal Seattle bettors getting those points). Thus, the risk takers have no exposure and make the "juice," which is the 10 percent betting fee as a locked-in profit.

This is not underwriting but rather a sure-fire way to make money for the gaming boys. It is not fraud, because everything is disclosed up front. The bettors are nothing but gamblers, meaning they have no control of the outcomes. Disgruntled bettors will always claim they've been screwed by Vegas because they know how to set the line and have insider knowledge. No...they just have great communication technology utilizing centralized computer systems. Gaming officials can have London bettors offset those in Tokyo. They can balance both sides of the bet so that there's no downside, only a profitable upside.

I am a risk taker, and in the insurance world as a CEO, I had decision-making power and thus became an underwriter. I established a premium rate to be charged to the student. Yes, I had to have the insurance company underwriters sign off on it, but my reputation proceeded me as being able to set profitable rates. My track record of over forty years was like a hall of fame coach: 245 wins, 100 losses, and 5 ties. This meant I was going to win and be profitable 70 percent of the time.

Insurance company underwriters knew little about the student-health industry, always wanting to challenge me on decisions, but invariably I proved to be right. My reputation preceded me. There were no statistical, actuarial tables to back me up, and therefore, I became the guru. This is also why I wanted a piece of this action. I wasn't my father or someone who established the premium rate and then wasn't part of the final result. I wanted to deposit a profit-sharing check into my bank account or write one to cover the underwriting loss. This is where the rubber meets the road.

Over the years, I've explored all kinds of ways to take on risk: off-shore companies, owning my own reinsurance company, and using the LOC (letter of credit) method, which was backing up the risk with personal collateral. In any event, I wanted to sit on the same side of the table as the big boys, the carriers and reinsurers with billions of capital dollars to play with. I always had to meet the challenge of the "yuppie greenhorn carrier underwriters."

Many times, just to stay in the game, I had to take (carve out) risk on my own. As an example, American University's health-center director wanted to place a transgender benefit into its policy for the 2008–09 school year. We had no support or prior experience for this kind of coverage. The risk pool, carrier and reinsurers, did not want to cover it, so I decided to do it myself on a "carve out." First, I had to break down the coverage to be offered: (1) consultation, (2) hormone shots, and (3) surgery. I decided to limit my exposure to exclude surgery and put a cap on the benefit of $5,000. Then I made some heroic assumptions.

- **6,000**   **Total students**
- **3%**   **will seek coverage**
- **$1,500**   **average payout/claim**
- **$270,000**   **projected claims**
- **$360,000**   **gross up premium-75% target loss ratio**
- **$60**   **cost per student**

Figure 6. Transgender underwriting model

My risk-pool partners then required me to put up an LOC for a third of the risk in exchange for half the claims' profit. The LOC was for $90,000. The actual runout by 2010 was slightly less than $100,000, so my profit sharing was approximately $85,000 plus 15 percent of the total premium for the administration that the operating company received. So all told, I made about $140,000 for underwriting the transgender benefit.

The risk partners had very little downside—only if their share of claims went over $180,000 and they shared equally in the profit. If the overall account profitability was off plan, that negated the carve-out terms. Their position with me, since I didn't have a billion-dollar-net-worth company, was, "If you want to do it, here are the terms on your underwriting"—which I assisted in determining—"take it or leave it."

I made a lot of deals like this and was successful more often than not. Plus, it gave me a gunslinger reputation with the risk partners. It was hard to find my equal in the marketplace; therefore, my services and ability to place business were in demand.

WHY AM I A RISK TAKER?

- First, I love the excitement of doing something others won't attempt for fear of failure or loss.
- Second, the power of negative is stronger than positive, and thus the rewards are inversely proportionate.
- Third, risk takers are game changers and set new strategies for the market or, many times, for the world.
- Finally, I get to ask myself, "Did the risk sharing benefit others?" If so, I know that God is involved in the process.

Take the risk! It is so worth it, otherwise you miss out on the promise of the future.

MY COMPANY EVOLUTION

Early on, Keystone Financial Corporation was my dream and was structured like a mini Ling-Temco-Vought (LTV): a mega-large holding company run by entrepreneur Jim Ling and that bought companies like Braniff International Airways, National Car Rental, Wilson & Company, and Jones and Laughlin Steel. At one point, LTV was one of the forty biggest industrial corporations.

I had bought the stock of Keystone in 1983 from my former partners, Edwin Norton and Ellison Miles, by exchanging my ownership in a luxury box at the old Texas Stadium (never missed a Cowboys home game in nine years), a third ownership in an office building, and some cash. Keystone was the holding company, owning 100 percent of the stock in Keystone Life and Keystone Casualty. Keystone Life was chartered to write life and health business, and Keystone Casualty was chartered to write property, auto, and health business. They were both licensed to write business in fourteen states. I had the structure for megabuck growth, just not the capital and surplus (a.k.a. C&S, or net worth). My A.M. Best rating was B, so I couldn't compete where A paper was required.

I tried many financial strategies to increase the net worth. A.M. Best had ratio tests tied to ratings. The critical one was premium to net worth, or "5–6 to 1," meaning five to six dollars of written premium to one dollar of net worth. Thus, $2 million net worth would only allow $10–12 million of premium to be written.

So the question was, how to get more capital? I did year-end reinsurance, where I would cede (transfer) life reserves for capital. This was similar to the stock tax straddles of the 1980s, dealing with puts and calls at year end. The effect was a year-end loss that could be reclaimed in the new year. In later years, the IRS prohibited these financial juggernauts. However, in business, It was all about making the year-end snapshot of the balance sheet look stronger.

Also, I sold surplus debentures to a business associate, Jan Tyler. He was a CPA and a smart, insurance-savvy guy, who was innovative in financial matters. We hit it off, but Jan wasn't going to give away anything. This was like rent-a-capital. Capital was paper infused (debenture) for a period of two to three years, paying a premium interest rate. The fact that the capital couldn't be withdrawn for a specified period would tally as net worth and, thus, the precious A rating. My goal was to write $100 million in premium using reinsured 65 percent quota share, which would require $6 million in capital and surplus, or $4 million more than I held currently via accounting gymnastics. Although it was a numbers game, the cost of year-end rent-a-capital and interest on debt or surplus debentures put a sizeable dent in my profitability.

In 1986, my downfall was being enticed into writing a large block ($90 million) of small-group health business. The two guys who brought the block of business to me needed a carrier, could accept my paper and rating, and were willing to pay a 6 percent fronting fee and a 33 percent share of the profits. Of course, there was a guaranteed history of profitability backed up by computer reports, which were, as it turned out, bogus. Additionally, as I learned later, the two guys, Milt Wilkerson and John Bogle, had flipped business like this in the past. When your only concern is your commission base and the lifestyle it affords, then profitability is totally secondary.

The book of business lost more than $10 million before I could pull the plug, wiping out my fronting fee plus almost $5 million of my precious remaining capital. I had been taken to the cleaners by some crooks in a segment of the market I knew little about. Da, dumb me. *Go not where it is murky.* (I'm not sure if that was Confucius, but the axiom probably predated his 551 BC time frame in practice.)

I was left with a $15-million block of college accident and health and K–12 accident business, along with the sick financial condition of my companies. Student health had always been my bread and butter, and I now vowed to stick strictly with the business I knew and never venture to business or products where I did not have an innate knowledge. Previously, I had never connected the dots on the ostrich business versus student health. I had just figured the Midas touch was in my genes.

So I had to find a buyer for my companies. I knew several business executives in the field. I went to an old friend, a mergers-and-acquisitions talent, Keith Tucker. A former PM&M partner, he had moved on to partner in a private venture capital investment company, the Stevens Company. Keith introduced me to Ron Jenson, who owned a public holding company, UICI, that in turn owned several insurance companies. We structured a purchase of my life and casualty companies, leaving me to head up a new student-insurance division (SID) of his holding company.

About all I salvaged were jobs for a hundred people and the ability to go forward. Jenson gave me little authority and obviously favored other executive personnel within his hierarchy. He said I was tainted due to running my companies into financial calamity. He was not to be trusted, and I quickly realized I couldn't work with him. I resigned and had less than $250,000 to launch something new. A pastor friend of mine, Keith Kraft of Elevate Life Church, gave a moving sermon on life and how God plans it. The message was this: *Everything good or bad has an end. It's the new beginning that's important.*

After completing the sale of Keystone Financial Corporation, where I was chairman and 100 percent stockholder, and exiting Jenson's UICI, I started a computer-networking company as an authorized Novell reseller. I bought a shell company in 1987, an S corporation, for next to nothing from Chris and Nancy Smith, which was designated as Chrina Corporation. Chrina got me back to my first love: computer software. At the time, desktop networking was the cutting edge in technology. It encompassed having a central file server (beefed-up desktop) that connected to smart workstations, providing the mainframe approach while allowing task computing to the workers' desks.

At the time, desktops were in a price war, competing for more RAM and enhanced cycle-processing speeds. We could replace older mainframes and link operating systems and applications from file servers to desktops while backing up only the servers. It was a turnkey process for less money than they were paying their mainframes or had recorded on their books. I had some techies who knew their stuff, and I "networked" some of my old computer contacts for new sales.

The computer business always had one big shortcoming: it wasn't stable. Competition was fierce, loyalty of employees was minus ten, and new and cheaper hardware was coming to market nonstop. So I kept my fingers in the pie but continued my student-insurance business by hiring some integral personnel from Jenson's UICI. I hired key marketing talent for college and K–12, and as a result of the office space glut and downturn of 1988, I was able to rent approximately ten thousand square feet of prime first-floor, class-A lease space for less than five dollars a square foot.

I used my old insurance contacts to create a new business model, where I secured a carrier as a front for paper and risk and reinsurers as supporting risk, with myself in a risk-partner position with LOC backup. Chrina Corporation would be the marketing entity collecting and processing premiums. The flaw was we had to outsource claims processing. This needed to be under my control in order to provide exemplary service, which tied directly to marketing objectives.

My IT guy, Jim Caserotti, had worked for me for several years at Keystone and had written the premium/claims system for my old software company, Affiliated Computer Systems. These systems were written in COBOL, vintage 1962, but the software was specifically suited to the student business and gave us a marketing edge. However, I needed to be licensed as a third-party administrator to legally administer claims. Through the collaboration of two attorneys (mine and a former insurance commissioner), I got licensed in five states. Some states rebelled against a Texas S corporation, and for those I formed a Delaware C corporation (Newco) that could operate in the other states I wanted to market to. I changed the name of Chrina Corporation to Chrina Corporation d/b/a GM-Southwest and of Newco to GM-Southwest, Inc.—really invisible, just reacting to licensing requirements. We were good to go and, with new structure and seasoned personnel, would be a formidable force in the marketplace.

In 1999 I faced a major financial hiccup after my thirty-eight-year marriage ended in divorce, near disaster, and the Ostrich venture had gone south. I was substantially lighter in the pocketbook, and I needed to reboot my personal capital base. The last link in my corporate structure was to set up a separate company to strictly do underwriting for a fee, separating me from the operating company and claims payments. My plan commenced in 2000. First, I dusted off my old ostrich LLC, set it up with one employee—me—and changed the name to Student Insurance Diversified (SID), ironically after UICI's designation. Secondly, I established a defined-benefit retirement plan. And third, sold my GM-Southwest stock to key employees under an ESOP arrangement.

The overall stock-sale structure was as follows: one times GM-Southwest's annual gross income paid over five years. Total business at that time was $30 million in written premium, and GMS received a 15 percent commission, or $4.5 million gross income. Transaction details included $200,000 each of five years qualifying for capital gains tax treatment and a 2.5 percent override on GMS written gross premium. All total, this equated to $4.5 million over five years, with capital gains on 22 percent of the payments. Any sales growth would be a bonus.

This method allowed me the flexibility to maximize my contributions as an only employee to my retirement plan and to get paid a flat amount up front under capital-gains tax treatment and a cash flow over five years based on an override on all sales. Key employees in the business for many years, including my children, would own the company and give me a swan song for a graceful exit.

Per almost usual, the plan didn't go as outlined on paper. One of the employees, Karon Gidney, couldn't get along with my daughter after being in the plan for five years. Plus, all payments were not made to me because of other cash-flow requirements. I came secondary to business requirements. The disgruntled employee filed a lawsuit against me to force a buyout of her portion of the stock. The suit claimed breach of contract, with accusations of insider malfeasance, paying family members a salary for no work. Overall, it painted me a Shylock asshole. Gidney, an employee whom I had taught many underwriting skills, had no personal money in her stock purchase, as each year I had arranged for extra bonus money to be paid to the ESOT participants so they could pay their taxes and write a net check to me, according to agreement terms.

We settled the case in mediation after spending more than $350,000 in legal fees. Gidney cried her eyes out, as the settlement was $75,000, which could barely pay her legal bill, with no glory in trying to be part owner of a privately held company. Remember, "private" says it's only worth what someone else will pay for it. There's no public market index and no price-earnings ratio to gauge stock value. According to Confucius (remember, 551 BC), "For best value, minority owners need to be friends with others." Or that might have been his brother's statement…I'm uncertain!

After ownership transfers and final payment to me in 2007, I spent less time in the office, even though I had a fascination with reinsurance and just risk taking in general. I loved the thrill of setting a premium rate that was sellable and having to wait for two to three years of claims to run out to see if my underwriting was successful. It was not a gamble, as I had some control of the outcome, but a lot of variables and unknowns could come my way, and did they ever!

Quota-Share Reinsurance

Reinsurance has, for at least forty years, been an integral part of the student-insurance market. A fully insured product means that an insurance company's net worth is guaranteed to cover any and all losses supporting the underwritten premium rate. The insurance company's financial strength has to be rated A or better by the national rating service, A.M. Best. Most insurance companies seek partners in risk sharing, not wanting to take on risk in a market most know little about or have had poor results in (with little or no profitability) in the past. Reinsurers fill that void and use their papers (net worth and licenses) to support the risk involved.

This concept started centuries ago with Lloyd's of London insuring the cargos of ships crossing the Atlantic against loss due to the perils of nature, pirates, or just the soundness of the vessel itself. Lloyd's has been a pioneer in insurance and has grown over 325 years to become the world's market leader for specialist insurance.

In more recent times, an underwriter as part of a syndicate takes a piece or percentage of the risk, known as the *quota share*. So, a 25 percent equal quota-share agreement would be one-quarter risk sharing between the primary insurance company (carrier) and three separate reinsurers. Some student markets may have as many as fifteen partners, which indicates that no one reinsurer wants too much of the risk. They can't get hurt too badly but also don't stand to win much. This is a good way to enter a new and/or volatile market.

In the past, each syndicate was backed by individual wealth portfolios and with signature authority for claims. The individuals were aristocrats or even royalty who had substantial wealth and were good for any claims that may have exceeded the premiums collected. In recent years, some syndicates have not been well financed and have challenged filed claims, only to litigate the fine print of the policy. Lloyd's has had to use rated reinsurers to replace unscrupulous syndicates.

In any case, primary and reinsurance paper have to be quality companies in order to withstand any non-underwritten claims. Underwriting involves analyzing the potential risk and setting a rate that is a balance between making a profit and being able to sell it to the consumer or requesting party or broker.

Now comes the part I like the most: participating as a risk partner without being a reinsurance company. An admitted reinsurance company has to be licensed by the state and has specific capital and surplus requirements, usually in the hundreds of millions. Plus, it must be rated A. I didn't have a company that qualified. Initially, I personally sought a risk position behind the carrier's paper. I did this by posting a LOC from a designated bank for an agreed-upon risk above the target loss ratio, usually 20 percent. The cost with good banking relations was typically 1 percent of the LOC. Since the 2008 financial debacle, 100 percent collateral was required, so the bank had little or no risk. I had serious "skin in the game."

Here's an example of what I'm talking about: An account with five thousand students paying a $2,000 annual premium, a 25 percent quota-share agreement with an underwritten 75 percent target loss ratio, and a 20 percent excess claims fund would require a $375,000 LOC to be posted at an agreed-upon bank, with the carrier as payee.

Annual renewal required:
    Total Premium= $10,000,000
        Risk premium @ 25% share-   **$2,500,000**
        Loss ratio risk attachment (75%)   **$1,875,000**
        Excess 20%-   **$375,000**

Figure 7. Quota-share risk

So how to finance this arrangement? GM-Southwest commissions were typically 15 percent of the collected premium. This was for all marketing/administration to basically "turnkey" the business for the carrier. I performed the underwriting, which was subject to carrier approval. In this case, 3.75 percent would be added to the premium charged. So the only challenge was being able to sell the rate to the school.

This completed the risk-taking process, enabling my company to be a partner in the good fortune or profits. A realized 60 percent loss ratio on the example given would yield a $375,000 profit sharing to my company. Furthermore, the insurance company had approved an underwriting agreement, allowing an underwriting fee to be paid to SID. This was subject to audit, which was performed every six months, and any exceptions noted for remedy. There were none. *I was compliant with the carrier's legal department.*

The operating company (GM-S) had a profitability model of 25 percent, assuming expenses were controlled. My underwriting company had downside risk if the loss ratio was more than 20 percent over target, or a realized 90 percent loss ratio. In that case, I would lose the 100 percent posted collateral to the LOC, and losses higher than 90 percent would have to come from my personal resources. Thus, one definition of successful underwriting: "charge enough to avoid unexpected losses."

The good fortune was strictly a matter of a profitable runout of claims results. My underwriting company had zero involvement with paid claims, so there were no Department of Insurance regulatory violations dealing with risk and claims payments. Underwriters have suffered hefty fines for having conflicts of interest or influence on how claims are to be paid.

The obvious other side to this is that the student paid for the method. The counter is, no one else in the marketplace could offer a better rate because they couldn't spread the risk as I was able to do. Also, stable rates are not subject to big rate increases upon renewal. On the other hand, insurance companies often practice giving a rate reduction in order to secure the business and 20–25 percent increase on renewal. Nationwide did this with car insurance in 2011 to get a corner on that market. It happens all the time with large insurance companies, and because of this practice their reputations are drug through the mud.

CHAPTER 4

Marriage and Valenti International

MY FIRST WIFE, BARBARA, WAS a good woman and a great mother to my children. I believe she simply lost interest in herself and me. I felt, selfishly, that I deserved better and that I just didn't want us to grow old together. I suggested divorce, but she wanted to hold our marriage together, mainly for the value of family and our children.

As I described earlier, she actually went so far as potential suicide by telling me she had taken cyanide capsules, which resulted in a mad dash to the Greenville hospital twenty miles away and then a CareFlight to Baylor Hospital in Dallas. The emergency docs quickly determined that her story about the lethal pills was a hoax. All of the emergency personnel from that point on treated both of us as complete lowlifes; they were really *pissed*. I was embarrassed but also realized that Barbara really wanted me back. In my mind it was too late, and with the ostrich farming having gone down the tubes, I felt an urge for a new start.

In 1999, even before the divorce, my eyes were wandering, and although I didn't frequent bars and other places to meet women, I did go to a few happy hours at upscale bars after work and did visit with the ladies there. I never picked up anybody, and even though I got a couple of hugs and kisses, I'd gotten zero dates.

One evening after work, during a two-dollar-beer happy hour, a young lady caught my eye, and she acknowledged me in return. I went over to introduce myself and visit with her. At five foot five and 130 pounds and with brown hair, Kimi Skipper was young and pretty and had a smile that could light up the world. Her personality matched the smile, and after finishing my drink and needing to go (I had a condo nearby and liked to watch the six-o'clock news and microwave a bite to eat), I asked her for her telephone number. She said, "No, give me yours."

At eight that night, she called. We talked and agreed to meet for dinner the next night. At this point, I was spending Monday through Thursday in town running my insurance business and the balance of Thursday to Monday at my ostrich farm, which at this point was virtually depleted.) Kimi and I had a delightful dinner, and her personality came to life big-time. This sparked a series of short evening dates.

I always called my wife later in the evening and before bedtime. I didn't feel good about this betrayal but rationalized it as her fault. She didn't care about me. I had recently won a sales incentive trip to Tahiti and Bora-Bora with Countrywide Insurance; my wife and I went to one of the most romantic places on earth, and there were no fireworks or stars between us. As the trip wound down, I was sitting in LAX between flights with Barbara taking a smoke break when I called Kimi and realized her freshness and vibrancy were what I needed—or at least I thought so at that moment. I ordered flowers from the airport to be delivered to her that day and met with her on a secret rendezvous (at Morton's Bar) the next day.

Our relationship flourished, and I decided to make a change in my life. It was difficult, as my wife had given me many great moments and years, along with three wonderful, "couldn't ask for better" children. She had been my partner in life, be it personal or business, and had even helped me to dissect business problems. Subconsciously I know I was wrong, but I was actually selfish and wanted a younger woman who was dialed into me and worshiped my every move.

The divorce was messy, and my children were not happy with me. My ex-wife was pretty well set financially—about $2 million, including my new townhouse, where she chose to live. She tried to hang on to me (including faking that suicide attempt), but we couldn't reconcile.

Kimi and I decided to get married in Belize. The date was March 3, 2001. I made arrangements for a minister and a honeymoon cottage on the beach on Ambergris Caye, a coral island off the coast of Belize with a quaint little village called San Pedro. Everything was so beautiful, and Kimi and I had a great time together. I felt really close to her but realized she was very dependent on me and somewhat naïve and vulnerable.

We started our life in a small house I bought in Addison, Texas. I still had the ranch and went out on weekends to tend to what was left. Barbara's sister, Susie, was still living there as a helping hand, and I could rely on her to take care of most of the depleted-ranch chores. I paid her a small salary and health insurance. She lived in the house that had originally been built by Barbara's parents on land I owned. They had moved to Texas after retirement to help us with the flourishing ostrich business. Her mother developed ovarian cancer, which quickly got the best of her. Rex, her dad, wanted to move back to Omaha, Nebraska, to a retirement community. Susie had a teenage son who also had been involved in the ostrich business. It all worked out, providing a good solution until I could sell the ranch and clean up loose ends from my first marriage.

Kimi and I decided to have a child. She had no children of her own, and it seemed like a good idea for our new union to translate to a family, which was very important to me. I remember thinking about my age when our planned baby would graduate from high school. I was sixty-one. Kimi thirty-seven, which was the same age as my oldest daughter

Tracy. My health was stellar at this point, and I felt a little bulletproof, which is never prudent under these types of circumstances.

During this time, we traveled some. Kimi was a paralegal for prestigious Addison law firm, and I was trying to rebuild my assets in my insurance company, which had somewhat taken a back seat to the ostrich business. I set up a small company, Legal-Jazz. Kimi worked on a contract basis for more than one firm; she could bill just like the legal beavers. With her talent and using my business acumen, she quickly could bill in the six-figure category with no overhead expenses.

The birth of our child, Tate Thomas Gutschlag, on September 7, 2002, put a halt to Legal-Jazz, but what a proud papa he made me. I was in the delivery room, cut the umbilical cord, helped clean him, and held him as a most precious boy. I felt so connected to him, more than with any of my other children. Years back I'd had to wait in a "dads' room," with the delivering physician coming in wearing scrubs and stating, "It's a healthy, beautiful baby girl/boy. No problem!"

Figure 8. Kimi Rae Skipper and Tate

Our new family started in glorious fashion. I had sold the ranch, along with all my equipment, livestock, and remaining ostriches. My insurance business was flourishing, and I had bought a new home, a ranchette on eight and a half acres in Aubrey, Texas. It was rural but close to the big city. I loved this house, as it had so much potential. It was only three years old, which was new compared to the ranch house and the other house in Addison. Initially I had a beautiful pool installed and constructed a carport connected to the former garage. This was eventually converted into a living area with a bath. The outbuilding housed my tools and leftover farm equipment, a small tractor, mowers, saws, etc. I also converted one of the barns into a workout facility. I gave up jogging, as we were in the country and 5:00 a.m. lighting was not good (I ran in the early morning hours). Also, my arthritic knee no longer responded well to hard surfaces. So I started running the treadmill after thirty-seven years of running five days a week on pavement.

Life was good, but Kimi was experiencing some postpartum depression and joint pain that we thought resulted from a rough delivery of Tate. We saw several doctors, and she was prescribed Enbrel for rheumatoid arthritis at $25,000 a year and psychiatry appointments for depression. Here it must be mentioned that Kimi had a low tolerance for pain of any kind. Her fear of childbirth and wanting to double-check on spinal blocks and how soon they worked led to prescriptions for hydrocodone and oxycodone. Well, and yes…she got hooked big-time. She doctor shopped to get more drugs and even falsified a renewal of a prescription I'd gotten when I had cosmetic eye surgery.

Kimi was not a big drinker and had a low tolerance to alcohol. But now she was drinking a lot more wine than usual. The combination of pain killers and alcohol turned her into a different person. Initially, she did a good job of hiding her addiction and/or consumption. But eventually her personality changed to be argumentative, short in temperament, and in some ways downright mean. Her care for Tate was not up to par, but between the both of us, Tate was fine.

She finally got arrested for falsifying prescriptions and was sentenced to three months in a drug-rehab center in Wilmer Hutchins, Texas. Tate and I would drive down on Saturday mornings to visit her. He was so cute and so happy to see her (and she him). I took classes about enabling an addict and was surprised to learn just how many times I had enabled her. My experience with drugs was zero—never even smoked a joint. I was a strict beer/wine guy and could always hold it.

When Kimi got out of the drug treatment center, she wanted to resume working while Tate remained in childcare. She had many legal contacts and quickly found another job. Tate was a very social kid and totally enjoyed daycare. Everything seemed fine until I got a call from her boss. He wanted to visit with me. The meeting revealed that Kimi was sneak drinking alcohol on the job. He did not want to fire her but was concerned about his client liability. I worked out an arrangement in which Kimi could go to a six-week drug rehab (on my insurance) if he would hold a job for her when she got out.

He went for it, but Kimi couldn't shake the temptations of drugs and alcohol. We tried several treatment centers in Grapevine, Dallas, and Center, Texas. Kimi could teach the course, but she couldn't say no. I always took Tate with me to those visitations. I didn't like their format: allow smoking till your lungs collapsed, go to school during the day, and sneak drugs in at night. It was a *sham*!

Kimi and I decided to call it quits with our marriage after child protective services got involved and I had to attend regular meetings with them. I bought her a small house ($250,000), gave her some cash, and got joint custody of Tate. We continued this arrangement until it became obvious that she couldn't take care of Tate, as she was not trustworthy. A crowning point was when the daycare called and asked me to come immediately. The police were there, as Kimi had picked up Tate drunk, putting him on her lap as she drove out of the center. They'd stopped her and called the cops. I told the police I'd take her home to avoid a trip downtown and more records.

The next day I called my lawyer to petition the court for full custody. No problem. Granted. Kimi lost the house, lost jobs, came out to my house periodically to visit Tate, left empty wine bottles in hidden places, sought more treatment, and finally disappeared. At this point, I didn't look for her. I'd taken a *risk* and lost with her but gained unmeasurably with a son.

After my second divorce, I realized I might not have everything figured out when it came to picking a mate. So I flew out to Rancho Santa Fe, California, to meet with Irene Valenti, president of the prestigious, world-renowned match-making firm Valenti International. Their statement was *"The more you have to offer, the harder it is to find someone special"*. Her offices were ostentatious, and she was dressed to the nines. Irene was about sixty—not particularly gorgeous, but attractive, with all the right accessories. She had a staff of psychologists, and I was assigned to one for my initial interview and ongoing contact. I had already taken some personality tests online, so they had a jump-start on who I was. Long/short, we (Irene, her staff, and I) hit it off, and they promised me success and everlasting happiness with the dream lady of my life. Their fee was $20,000 up front and the same amount when I was married. Later, I found out that these rates vacillated depending on who you were and what they could get away with. One lady said she had paid $100,000 up front!

The way it worked was that the office manager and all-around gopher, Robert, would call me with an introduction. He would only tell me generalities: age range, height, hair and eye color, and a little background (i.e., home location, vocation, and general interests)—no last name or weight. Bob and I would then establish a meeting location and timing. From there, it was a matter of my showing up and then Ms. Special walking in the door of my life. Keep in mind, the staff of PhDs believed they had found my Cinderella.

My first intro was Pat. We were to meet in the bar at the Ritz Carlton in Laguna Beach, California. I checked into the hotel the night before, only five days before Christmas. I got the lay of the land and geared up for my first "made in heaven" introduction. Many hours and three beers later, I still sat in the bar. Bob called my cell and said that Pat had had an emergency and had to cancel. I was livid and told Bob that this was bullshit and that I wanted her to call me *muy pronto* so I could hear firsthand about her emergency. Bob did what I asked, and Pat called. I let off some steam about protocol and correctness, but Pat was gone forever. Bob, who had undoubtedly experienced this before, had a backup, an "intro number two," who could meet me the next night: same bar and same time.

This time in walked the attractive Denise Weatherspoon—fiftyish, five foot five, guessing 110 pounds—with her chauffeur. We excused the driver and had a drink. Then we drove down to another hotel bar she was hot on, had another drink, and then went back to the Ritz for dinner. We danced to an orchestra playing Christmas music and had a very good time.

She wanted to bring her mother, who was visiting from Hawaii, to meet me for breakfast in the morning. We met, had breakfast and a good conversation, exchanged phone numbers and addresses, and kissed good-bye. We planned to circle back for another meeting on my turf.

Bob had called before I retired that last night, asking about Denise but said the real reason he was calling was that Irene was most apologetic about the missed "intro number one." She wanted me to meet one of her favorite ladies who had just joined Valenti, and was I game? Where? Las Vegas, tonight, three days before Christmas! Bob had my itinerary for flights and booked me into the Four Seasons. I was to meet Carolyn in the bar at 6:30 p.m. I hung out in the lobby, discreetly tucked behind a huge flowerpot, to get a first peek at "intro number three" before I made my entrance. Carolyn Chesnutt, a dance instructor, was fiftyish, five seven, 115 pounds, trim, and attractive with a mink shawl wrapped around her bare shoulders. We had a drink in the bar, then dinner, and then caught a cab to the Bellagio, where we gambled at the craps table, played roulette, drank in the bar, and talked. We took a cab back to the Four Seasons at 2:00 a.m. She had to teach a class six hours later, and I had a flight to catch, so we kissed, exchanged phone numbers and addresses, and agreed to meet again in Dallas.

On separate occasions, I met with both Carolyn and Denise in Dallas. They stayed at my house each time, and we dined at expensive restaurants I knew well, had sex, and talked about everything. But at the end of the day, I couldn't feel the connection with either of them becoming a future. Carolyn was kind of quirky, at least for me, and Denise was California beach gal who didn't grasp how the real world worked. Money was no object, she had a gay son, and her sense of values was not there. She had flipped a house in Newport Beach and made $750,000, while holding it for only three months. She figured herself as a real-estate guru, while in fact California housing prices were insane and supply-demand ratios were flipped, which was why the housing market turns were no-brainers. Relative values hurt the real home owners, but escalating values were a prize for investors. She wanted me to invest with her, but I couldn't sell myself on California people or their housing market. I thought the risk wasn't worth it, as I would be an absentee investor. This doesn't work unless you're lucky, and I'm not. We stayed in contact as friends and would talk on the phone and share a glass of wine long distance.

Figure 9. Valenti introduction number three, Denise Weatherspoon

One introduction resulted in an engagement ring—that story is somewhat embarrassing, but here it is. Later, intros came will more detail. Joy Lincoln was a fit model with a PhD. She was forty-nine years old, five seven, 115 pounds, blue-eyed, and blond, with a gorgeous body and face, too. She had a nine-year-old boy and hit it off with Tate, and he liked both of them. She mentioned having some money problems, but she lived in Highland Park, a really prestigious neighborhood within Dallas proper, and drove a Mercedes. She had a full-time job at Highland Park ISD as a psychologist making $80,000 and a pending settlement on a lawsuit she had against a student who roughed her up in the hallway because he didn't like the way she had talked to him. The district had insurance coverage for such instances, and she stood to be awarded about $500,000.

We dated and traveled some. She pushed for a home in Highland Park and to keep mine for our country home. She wanted an engagement ring and said that having sex without one is bad luck. I really didn't buy this but said I would buy her a commitment ring and that if things didn't work out, it would be returned. I had researched the law in Texas on this, and the term "engagement" meant she could keep it if she walked.

Anyway, wouldn't you know she had just the store and jeweler, and the ring was to die for, five carats, round, VVS2-H. I negotiated a great deal and bought it for $33,000. Our relationship started to crumble, particularly after I nixed the Highland Park house. I asked for the ring back, and basically she gave me a "finders keepers" argument. She sued me for possession of the ring. Depositions and $20,000 in legal fees resulted. She paid me $15,000 for the ring, and we settled the case.

As a follow-up two years later in 2010, I changed cardiologists, and my new doctor was actually married to Joy and living in a Highland Park mansion. He knew my history with Joy and wondered if I thought there was a professional conflict. I pondered it and said, yes, I wasn't comfortable and that I believed he had been behind the scenes during the lawsuit, paying the bills. Her cost had to have been in the $40,000s, and on an $80,000 salary for a $33,000 ring? No way! Also, I had heard she had been tricking around while I was dating her. I changed cardiologists and never looked back for Joy.

Next and in 2007, I was introduced to Candace Gibson, a pediatric cardiologist working at Johns Hopkins Hospital in Baltimore. She was five foot five and fifty-eight years old and had red (dyed) hair. We talked several times on the phone, and she struck me as someone who was very bright but also conversant on many subjects. Intellectually, I felt a connection. She wouldn't exchange pictures, as she indicated it wasn't ladylike. I had to agree, but it also triggered my curiosity about this woman of many interests.

We agreed to meet at the Baltimore airport and go from there. We connected in baggage claim. She was not as beautiful as some of my intros had been, but she was attractive in her own way and definitely a lady of grace. We drove in her Jaguar convertible to the Tysons Corner Four Seasons Hotel.

She had a reservation for a suite, prepaid on her Amex card. We decided to have our bags sent up to the room and go to the bar. Candace was very open and said she was uncomfortable and nervous about having sex. She said this was a first for her for this type of rendezvous. She had been married and had one son by that marriage, which had ended because of his infidelity. She then married a navy captain, but they just weren't on the same page intellectually. No children. After two glasses of Chardonnay, she decided it was time for exploration. We had some great sex, and she certainly knew what she was doing, whether by experience or book learning—and I would bet on the latter.

The next day we went to her house overlooking the South River, not far from Annapolis, where she had graduated from the naval academy and had been a pediatrician in the navy for twenty years (she had a full retirement in her future). She had planned a neighborhood party where I could meet the neighbors and her brother's family, who lived nearby. She was an excellent host and made me feel very comfortable, boasting to the attendees what a successful businessman I was and detailed many of my prestigious university contacts.

Candace loved the game of golf, and we traveled and played a range of courses in DC, Homestead, and elsewhere. Most of the time, Tate traveled with us, and with the help of sitters and resort child activities, we could all do our own things and be happy. She was unbelievable with Tate, as a former pediatrician and caring doctor. We traveled to meet her parents and other family members at Thanksgiving. We enjoyed Christmas in St Michaels (the Christmas-light town) in Maryland.

Soon after, we traveled to Hilton Head, South Carolina, visiting her aunt and uncle, who had a lovely place there. We were all at dinner, and Candace stated to everyone, "Don't you think I'll be the grande dame wife of Mr. Gutschlag?" Everyone looked at me for affirmation, and I, caught off guard, fluffed it off—or just didn't smile, nod my head, or give a thumbs-up. Later, Candace addressed me in private and was really annoyed that I hadn't been more positive about our intentions to marry. She said, "This is what Valenti is all about, finding a lifelong mate—not just screwing around."

I realized then that I didn't like a woman with a dogmatic approach. I had been a CEO for so many years, and any subordinate who approached me in that matter was either terminated or demoted. I always had a difficult time separating my business life from my personal one. I didn't make friends easily. I was much more business than social.

We continued to see each other until the morning after a big Super Bowl party in Savannah, Georgia. We were both scheduled to depart that morning to return to our respective workplaces/homes. The alarm went off at 5:30 a.m. to catch 7:00 a.m. flights. She started screaming about how we needed to get up and get going. She needed the bathroom first. Needless to say, I just didn't say, "OK, my dear." We traveled to the airport in silence and departed with a light kiss, and I was never to see her again.

We had planned to go to Disney World in Orlando along with Tate. I had prepaid the entire trip. Sure, I contacted her, but she was done and basically so was I. Tate and I spent a great four days at Disney World by ourselves, and it was a great experience for him. Candace contacted me one other time, after she had moved to Dallas and taken a position at Children's Medical Center. She called and said, "Let's have a beer and catch up."

I replied, "Well, I'm going with someone else now, and I don't believe it would be gentlemanlike."

During my time with Valenti, I had twenty-six introductions over six years. I met fifteen of them. Several other intros were by phone, as distances for whatever reason hindered any in-person meetings. Nine intros I saw more than once, and there were three that lasted more than six months, where the woman asked me to marry her.

I handled my parenting duties with Tate during this time with the help of daycare, Montessori school, and some great babysitters when I traveled. He always met and interacted with my lady friends. His sparkling smile and attitude was always refreshing to me and my barometer as to "how he was doing."

My last, intro number twenty-six, was Brenda Golden: sixty years old, five six, 115 pounds, blue-eyed, blond, church-music performer.

I was a "risk taker," someone who risks loss in the hope of gain or excitement. I had realized both and probably a 60/40 percentage split.

Figure 10. Dad and Tate

I was introduced to Brenda through a phone number from Valenti on June 3, 2009. They said she was a beautiful southern girl with musical talent and that she was financially secure. We started our long-distance romance (Houston/Dallas) by talking numerous times. She seemed so sweet, soft spoken, religious, and even somewhat naïve. I had already planned a trip back to Omaha to visit with some of my old fraternity brothers and play some golf, and therefore, I was unable to immediately see Brenda in person. I asked for pics, and she sent me some really risqué photos. One showed huge Dolly Parton cleavage, and all were very sensual. This was so different from the image in my mind via our phone calls. I had to meet this woman!

Figure 10. Brenda Carol Golden

I arranged a trip to Houston, booked the Clear Lake Hilton, flew to Hobby Airport, and cabbed to her house in Friendswood. I knocked on the door, and this soft voice said, "Come on in; door's open." Her dog, a bichon, met me, jumping and all excited. Brenda walked toward me down a long hallway, dressed in a black cocktail dress. She was indeed beautiful, and her pictures hadn't lied.

We had a glass of wine at the kitchen bar and talked very freely about many subjects: family, weather, Houston, etc. We took the only car in the three-stall garage, a four- or five-year-old Jaguar, to Perry's Steakhouse, a local Houston chain soon to open in Dallas. We got there, she introduced me to the manager and bar help, and we had a glass of Chardonnay. She was obviously a regular. We dined in a private booth, and she told me some of her financial woes and that the house she was living in might be repossessed.

We got ready to leave, and she took what I thought was an extra length of time in the ladies' room. When she exited, I was standing in the hallway and noticed she had just applied makeup and ruby red lipstick. I kissed her on the smacker, and she said, "Oh, don't get lipstick on you." To me, this was her gracious way of not complaining about my messing up what had taken her a long time to apply. Definitely she did not appear to be self-centered.

We traveled back to her home, or where she was living, and she proceeded to show me the whole house and its furnishings—all high-end, beautiful stuff. She said the "man" and owner lived upstairs, and she downstairs. It was clearly laid out that way: his space and her space. She explained he was a real-estate developer who had fallen on bad times with the 2008 and current housing crunch. She had sold homes for him and had been with him off and on at social events to promote his company. She liked to explain it as he liked a lady on his arm to showcase. He was very generous, and they had a platonic relationship that had spanned eighteen years. It did fall out of the conversation that he would like to talk with me about buying the house and that it was a really good financial opportunity. I said, fine, I would do so.

Brenda was very upbeat and wanted to show me her cabana, which was built to be hurricane-proof and as an emergency shelter. It was very impressive, and as we reached the top of the winding staircase to the bedroom loft, she stopped, and we kissed very passionately. It wasn't very long before her dress was circled around her ankles, and I noticed she wasn't wearing a bra or patties. She had been completely naked under that dress. I couldn't get my trousers over my boots, so she gave me oral sex. We had sex another time that night on her family-room sofa—this time, vanilla type. It was great; she was very sensual and had a beautiful body. I didn't want to call a cab for the Hilton, but she thought it better for me to sleep in a guest bedroom named appropriately "the African room," decked out with artifacts and expensive furniture, African style. I presumed it had all come from a trip she had made. The next morning, she greeted me in the kitchen with coffee and pastries, saying, "Well, I guess we did everything—now what do we do?"

Do it? Did we! We traveled to New York, New Orleans, San Diego, and Las Vegas, dined in the best restaurants, and my introduction to her shopping was…well, nothing I had ever experienced and got my attention, as she knew the best designers, shops, and labels.

Figure 11. Sparks restaurant in NYC-December 2009

On an early trip to the "Big Easy," we stayed at the Windsor Court, a four star or maybe five, but ratings are a farce. This place was nice. We were getting to know each other outside of sex, and I caught her cold on two questions at separate times. First, I said, "What is it *you* love about me?" She stumbled, and I playfully persisted.

She said, half laughing, "Your hands." I never liked that answer.

The second question was the next day after sex, in the sitting room of our suite. I said, "Why don't I just give you $75,000, and we go our separate ways? You have financial issues, and I may not be able to solve them all." She almost pretended to not hear me and just dismissed the question. Later that evening, over wine and dinner a Galatoire's (we always drank one or two bottles of wine at a meal), she said to me, "Whatever our differences or difficulties are, my love is unconditional." This really stuck with me as on par with a wedding vow: "For better or worse, as long as you shall live."

I met with Kevin Samuel Price, the man of the house, at Maguire's restaurant in Dallas. By this time, I had drilled Brenda down about this guy living on the second floor and using her arm for social/business purposes. They had traveled numerous places together (Africa for one) and had sex...I never could pin down the number of times, but certainly more than once. They had talked marriage, but Kevin was a confirmed bachelor, and, after witnessing Brenda's family, complete with screaming grandkids, decided the commitment would interfere with his penchant for hunting. Our meeting was business and what I consider an honest portrayal as Kevin knew it. He had everything laid out on what he wanted and what was in it for me. The house, 3361 Prince George in Friendswood, had a mortgage of $425,000 and a second of $150,000. He itemized in detail the add-ons at $325,000, including the hurricane-proof cabana, special painting, pool, and oversize closet for Brenda. He had an appraisal of $975,000.

Here was the deal: he would set me up with his lawyer to buy the house out of foreclosure on the courthouse steps for the primary mortgage, then Price would walk the second, and I would give him some split on selling the house at anything over $650,000. When I sold it, I'd make an up-front $225,000, plus the split. For the deal, he wanted an up-front $50,000 so he could move out of the house, disappear from the IRS (as he had major difficulty with them), and send us wedding flowers. He said Brenda was mostly low-key and had a lovely mother and a son he didn't know what to do with. I countered with the house deal as OK up front, but with no commitment on a profit split at any price (I could include this later at my discretion). I wanted for the $50,000 up front all of the house furnishings to serve as collateral and a purchase leaseback. He said the furnishings were worth $400,000. I later found a file in his old desk, which was now mine, that showed he had been trying to sell the same furnishings for $200,000. No takers.

We were off to the races, and Brenda and I were married at the Ritz-Carlton in Houston, April 9, 2010, with her mother officiating. Her mother indicated she had been a pastor in the Assembly of God church for fifty-five years. I took her word for it.

Brenda sang in the bar after our ceremony and dinner. She is one talented performer. This was the first time I'd ever heard her sing, even though her girlfriends and Kevin had said, "Boy, does this gal have some vocals." My brother and his wife, Kathey, along with Brenda's daughter and her kids, and Brenda's disabled son, Jonathan, attended. Her other son, Derek, and his family did not. Nor did my other children.

We were off to honeymoon in Monte Carlo, Southern France, Paris, the Black Forest of Germany, and most of Italy—a total of twenty-five days.

Figure 12. The two of us on honeymoon in Monte Carlo

We had planned to get remarried in Rome and Neuschwanstein, Germany. This was all about total commitment and the nuances of European marriage for prosperity sake. We were newlyweds, but I quickly found that Brenda took two hours to go anywhere. We were on a tour with twenty-five other folks from all over the United States. A typical day included bags at our hotel-room door at 7:00 a.m. and the bus loading at 8:00 a.m., and then we were off to sight-see, have lunch, see more sights, have a dinner of our choosing, and most days, bed down in a new hotel. Actually, we were in ten hotels during our trip. Brenda had trouble with the pace, and she hadn't packed for cold weather. (April in Europe can be chilly.) She ended up buying $2,000 worth of clothing. And she made me feel as if I was the one who had packed her bags with all the wrong clothes.

We saw so many sights and had sex everywhere possible (a roof-top restaurant on the Italian Rivera was the impossible). Our trip got stalled because of the volcano eruption in Iceland. All the air traffic was grounded for five days while we were in Paris, for shame. As a result, we missed going to Germany. Bren got sick in Paris, but she continued to try and meet the rigorous schedule. She showed her perseverance and quest for shopping. She could buy fancy stockings for $500 and think nothing about it. "You buy nice things for those you love," she would say.

All in all, the trip was one in a lifetime. She recovered from her illness but got a bladder infection, and her mother said, "I guessed it—too much sex."

When we returned home, we continued our lifestyle of commuting between Dallas and Houston. I bought the house at foreclosure for $411,000 and the furniture to give Kevin a safe landing outside of my home and away from Brenda. My attorney handled the transactions, as I never knew when it might be questioned.

I hired an architect to design addition plans for my homestead house on eight and a half acres. I was looking to house Bren and me, Tate, Brenda's mother, and her son Jonathan. That meant we needed five bedrooms, including guest quarters. Brenda pretty well shot that idea down. She wanted a new house for us, and her mother and son could live in my older home. I found a beautiful oceanfront house plan on the Internet that we used along with my architect to customize some of my ideas and needs. Bren was of little help, as she couldn't visualize concepts from Houston, and when I showed her the draft plans, she said it made her dizzy. So I pretty much made all the decisions, along with the help of a $10,000 decorator I hired. The big move was going to take place August 11, 2011. I sold the Houston house for $620,000, net $570,000. Yes, you guessed it—a bad market and top of the neighborhood house. The fact she lived there with her mother/

son for twenty-three months at a cost of $5,000 per month (utilities and extraordinary maintenance expense) meant I actually lost money on the "Houston house deal," including my legal costs. So much for Kevin Price, who had disappeared, but I always wondered how. when you're running from the biggest sleuth—that is, the IRS. I think he just wanted out, and his concept to own was financed to the hilt. An example of his finance style: he bought a new Jaguar for Brenda, strictly on payments with low money down. He would make about three payments of $1,000 and let her drive for six months before repo came. She was clueless. He knew enough people so he could do it again. He had ways of correcting his credit report. Bren just liked driving new exotic cars and couldn't care less how it was financed.

I settled in with my third wife in September of 2011. The entire time from our first meeting in June 2009 until 2011 (twenty-eight months) had been a time-consuming journey, most of which I thoroughly enjoyed, but it took me away from my business, which allowed me to pay the bills...and lots of them.

Please be patient and see the conclusion in chapter 9.

CHAPTER 5

Victims

WHO'S THE VICTIM?

IN THE STUDENT-INSURANCE INDUSTRY, THE student appears to be victimized by the enterprise participants. They rely on fiduciary involvement, whereas these "helpers" have more self-interest than they'll admit to or care to discuss.

The students are mostly reticent in insurance-contract decisions, mainly because they don't understand one of the principles of insurance—which is to spread the risk to the point where the masses have access to more affordable rates. They want to focus on the sensationalism of a particular claim to exemplify inequality rather than what's for the overall good of all insured.

College administrators always profess student importance as their future, but most of them usually have "self" stamped on their foreheads. If insurance through add-on fees can benefit their budgets, or God forbid, a broker buys something personal for them, then their eyesight/vision becomes blurred. Brokers and agents are, by far, the worst when it comes to manipulation of the contract for self-serving benefits. They act as consumer advocates, but rarely have I seen the student being put first.

Insurance companies and their reinsurance partners have two priorities, which in both incidences are labeled "profit." They couldn't care less about the student; rather, they look to their marketing agent(s) to control the accounts and sell profitable premium rates. They appoint the agents by state to represent them, thus credentialing that mutual relationship. The companies have audit responsibility to certify compliance to their standards, which prohibits misrepresentation and any fraudulent deeds. However, their audits rarely include what information is being provided to the schools or the accuracy thereof. Suffice it to say insurance companies and their risk-bearing partners are culpable of any and all fraudulent charges. They choose to turn their heads if profit margins are being achieved or exceeded.

Finally, the student may be considered a victim, but many instances of a "good deal" are evident. The marketing agent, myself in many instances, would negotiate discounts with a provider's network that would not be accessible by the competition because of an "exclusive" contract. Therefore, these accounts and participating students received the best premium rates in the industry, regardless of the reporting presented.

This argument could be made in those unique circumstances: Should the risk taker be entitled to the profits without sharing with the insured? The policy issued was "fully insured," which contractually says the premium rate, once issued, cannot be changed, and all profit or losses are to be borne by the insurance company, period. Students have no right to the cake and then eating it, too. Student plight can only be determined on a case-by-case basis.[4]

On the following pages, I will provide some examples of fraud I saw firsthand and how it took place. Please note how the various parties in the enterprise took advantage of the victim, the student.

---

4 Obamacare has changed the refund provisions, but as I've described elsewhere, the tactics and reserve gymnastics that insurance companies utilize essentially negates this possibility.

Fraud #1

Victim: Student
Perpetrator: Agent/Broker of Record (BOR)
Accomplice: Student Health Director (SHD)
Process: Insurance company reporting is modified by the agent using Excel to duplicate format, font, and point size of an actual systems report to show better experience than actual.[5] The BOR shops several insurance companies to gain rates better than current premium rates. The BOR and SHD decide to take the difference in a combination of health-center fees and commissions.
Outcome: SHD has additional funds to spend at her discretion, and BOR increases personal income while student rates are unchanged. Everyone wins, except the student didn't understand the flow of funds or profit incentives. He paid the inflated premium. Deception and greed-based actions include money laundering, conspiracy, and wire fraud.

Specific Example

Setting: The broker of record, Angie White, has an exclusive BOR designation, meaning all competitive or any outside communication has to be processed through her before it is presented to Dr. Eileen Metcalf, director of the student-health center. Dr. Metcalf presides over a cost center with a school-year budget of $10 million. She reports to the vice chancellor of student affairs. Dr. Metcalf has an annual salary of $110,000, with a bonus based on 10 percent of the amount under operating budget. She relies on the

---

5 More premium and fewer claims equals an inviting, profitable loss ratio.

BOR for all insurance direction. Her employer is the students, and she has major fiduciary responsibility to them.

Meeting
Place and
Time: Student-health center at Georgia Tech, March 20, 2013 (Dr. Metcalf and Angie)

Purpose: Student-insurance renewal commitment for the school year 2013–14

It's a beautiful spring day. The azaleas are starting to come out, and the student union is bustling with activity. The meeting is on the first floor. Dr. Metcalf and Angie go back several years, when Dr. Metcalf was assistant SHC director for Central Florida College. They've hobnobbed, drunk good wine, and dined together—and of course, talked men, their favorite discourse. But they must portray a professional relationship.

"Good morning, Dr. Metcalf."

"Good morning, Ms. White."

"I love your nails—what color?"

"Oh, fuchsia," says the doctor.

"Wow, looks great on you! I haven't seen that bracelet before—exquisite!"

"Thank you, Angie; you're so kind."

"Well, I've got good news for you today."

"Please tell," says Dr. Metcalf.

"I finally got an experience report from our current insurance company, and while I had to 'doctor' the report so it shows favorable experience…"

"What do you mean, 'doctor'?" asks Dr. Metcalf.

"Well, you know those insurance companies and their IBNR reserves, always pumping up the claims from reality."

"Yes, Angie, what do we do about that?"

"Only one thing to do: remove some of the IBNR. It's all insurance-company profit anyway," says Angie.

"How?"

"I re-create the company report in Excel using the same font and point size, and change claims figures to where the overall loss ratio looks better. Then I can shop the report with other insurance companies for a better premium rate."

Dr. Metcalf says, "Angie, you're so smart. Thanks for helping me. What do we do next?"

"When we get renewal premiums back from the companies, I'll spreadsheet them and then make a decision on who to renew with."

"You can do all this?"

Angie says, "Hey, girlfriend, remember when I told you about the best steak house in NYC at the ACHA Convention last year?"

"Oh, yes," replies Dr. Metcalf.

"I not only told you about it, but we also dined there and had two great bottles of Far Niente Chardonnay. As a matter of fact, I'm already two steps up on this renewal. I got a quote yesterday from Nationwide at ten percent less than current rates."

"You are wonderful; you are so smart! Just like when you say, 'I've got just the man for you'…I never doubt it!"

"Now look at what else we can do!"

"Please tell!" says Dr. Metcalf.

"You know that portable X-ray machine you need and couldn't get approved in your capital-expenditure budget?"

Dr. Metcalf sighs. "Yes, and I'm sick about it."

"Let me take you through the math. The annual student premium here is about seven million dollars, covering six thousand students at about twelve hundred dollars per student per year. I can get a ten percent reduction in the rate by carrier shopping. Rather than reduce the annual rate for students, we simply add an administration fee on to the rate so you can get your X-ray machine."

Dr. Metcalf asks, "So the students aren't charged more than they are at present, and there's money to buy the X-ray machine. *Wow*, I like it!"

Angie asks, "How much is this machine?"

"Approximately five hundred fifty thousand."

"Well, we've got seven hundred thousand to play with (ten percent of seven million). Would you have a problem if I increased my commission for the difference? My expenses keep rising, my husband isn't working, and yes, we women carry the burden."

Dr. Metcalf agrees. "Sounds fair to me."

"I'll get additional quotes from UHC, BC/BS, Anthem, and Aetna. That way, your vice chancellor will love you."

"Angie, you're the best!"

Angie says, "I'll get back with you next week, and then we can lock it in. Also, I want you to try this spa over on Pernales Street. It's high-end, and their full-body massage is to die for. I've got a membership and have one free guest pass. It's yours."

Dr. Metcalf says, "Toodle-oo, see you next week, girlfriend!"

Bottom Line: False reporting just screwed the insurance company. The students don't get a break unless everyone gets free X-rays. The health-center director looks good to her boss for bonus potential and gets a free body scrub and an X-ray machine. Angie is the winner; she locked in a renewal and increased her commissions over an already-exorbitant number by $150,000. She can celebrate with her nonworking husband!

Fraud #2

Victim: Student
Perpetrator: Insurance Company
Process: The insurance company overstates IBNR reserve to justify higher rates and defer taxes. A growing business (a must) allows for the ability to inflate reserves. IBNR can include such factors as: (1) industry trends, (2) multiyear rate guarantees, (3) benefit changes, and (4) other factors. Reserves represent a liability to the insurance company. It can be multiyear reserves, as is the case with Obamacare (two partial school years within one calendar year).
Summary: Insurance companies can justify through reserves additional or higher rate increases and have the reserves signed off on by independent actuaries. No state insurance department will contest this, and therefore, excess profits or overcharging is within the insurance companies' prerogative. The victim is the student, who is paying deceptively high premiums and not sharing in the company profits. Fraudulent actions include deception, money laundering, and wire fraud.

Specific Example

Setting: Headquarter offices of Countrywide Life Insurance in a meeting to qualify the new book of student-health business
Business: Thirty-one accounts, approximately $25 million in annualized premiums, and fifteen thousand insured students
Attendance: Melissa Alverez, senior VP of the health division; Tom Dobbie, VP of health division; Mark Porker, VP of marketing; Steve Gabitch, account specialist; and John Gutschlag, CEO of GM-S, using a Power Point presentation regarding the book of business and the profitability of the respective accounts

I conclude my presentation by stating, "My lady and gentlemen, there you have it—a good solid block of thirty-one accounts, some twenty-five million dollars in new premiums, and last, but certainly not least, profitability!"

The room applauds.

Melissa says, "John, I need to attend another meeting, and I know your business is always good. I will join you for dinner tonight at Roma's. I'll let these gentlemen carry on for me. I vote affirmative, but Tom, get everything pinned down Countrywide-wise."

Everyone chuckles.

Steve Gabitch raises his hand. "May I, John?"

I say sure, recognizing Steve.

Steve asks, "The Virginia Tech account is very profitable—with a loss ratio in the fifty to sixty percent range. Can you retain the account?"

I say with confidence, "I've had it for twenty years and have an account rep, Jim Lane, who mother hens this account. He has a long-standing relationship with the risk manager. They drink and play golf together, know what I mean?"

Everyone nods his head.

Mark Porker says, "John, Lane must be screwing someone for that longevity."

I say, "Mark, you're always implying that women are involved. It's just about plain, old customer service."

Tom Dobbie comments, "John, my concern is keeping the competition from lowballing the rate and stealing it from you. The last thing I want to happen is to lose Tech and get stuck with a lot of accounts that are not that profitable. Mind you, John, our careers here at Countrywide are all about profitability. We are in business to make money and have no patience for losers."

I state, "Tom, I read you loud and clear, but you agree that pooling accounts allows for more premium on the books."

Tom says, "OK, but Tech is the key to the book of business. How do we keep them from demanding a rate reduction when their losses are in the fifties?"

I point to Steve. "Remember, Steve, when we talked about the software that adds the discounts to the paid claims, thus making the losses appear worse than they are?"

Steve nods his head. "Yes, this was developed by BC/BS of Virginia several years ago on the basis that discounts are proprietary and, according to the contract with the providers, can't be disclosed."

Tom says, "I love it! Screw the competition! We don't need them to let us do all this work, and then they ambush us with a lowball rate and steal the business. Screw 'em!"

Mark, who's a little brighter light than the others, says, "We have to be careful not to purposely mislead the schools—that's fraud."

Tom says, "Let's use IBNR reserves; that way we can do whatever we want to inflate the claims and blame it on the actuaries, if it is questioned. You know that those guys (the actuaries) will approve whatever we send them, and this is such a small piece of business compared to our other health premiums. It will get lost in the haystack." Tom reiterates, "We need profitable business and will protect it with our jobs."

Everyone says, "Yeah! Let's go have a celebratory drink and steak."

Mark says, "Drinks?"

Everyone laughs.

I say, "Hey, guys, not so fast. We're talking about profitable business. How does old John participate?"

Tom says, "Oh, you want to share with us?"

I say, "Absolutely."

Mark pipes up, "I've got a profit-sharing plan we did with a large broker in the Medicare supplement business. Basically, it shares two points on both sides of the target loss ratio. If it goes over, you pay us; if it goes under, we pay you. Two points max."

I say, "That's as good as you can do for a friend?"

Tom replies, "Let's talk further over those drinks that are sitting on the bar."

Everyone laughs.

Bottom Line: The insurance company will go all out to protect its profit; when it comes to sharing, it'll yield very little. The Tech account ran a 44 percent loss ratio. The target was 70 percent. They would give me 2 percent and keep 24 percent. The drinks produced memory loss. "The big insurance companies' mentality tends to be 'Take it or leave it.' But we at Countrywide deem you a partner extraordinaire."

I said under my breath, "Greedy SOBs," and moved the business to Aetna that year—with a point-for-point profit share. No limits. Screw Countrywide!

Fraud #3

Victim: Students

Perpetrators: Broker of Record (BOR) or Consultant

Process: The BOR receives the carrier experience data and modifies it to further enhance his or her role of need. Experience data may be withheld and available only to certain bidding entities. It can be changed to include administrative fees added to the premium or net. Premium can be shown as collected premium; thus, the admin fees cannot be determined, therefore making underwriting less than accurate. Brokers may rearrange experience data on a calendar-year basis, thus obliterating underwriting needs by school year.

Summary: BOR control of the contract is often tied to commission rates for whoever is awarded the business. This results in market control, fraud, and excess commission—where students overpay the cost of insurance.

SPECIFIC EXAMPLE

Setting: Mercer offices in Philadelphia

Participants: Principal Brian Hamlin, Associate Liz McAdory, and John Gutschlag, CEO of GM-S, in his Dallas office

Activity: We are exchanging a series of e-mails regarding Brown University's request for proposal (RFP). The incumbent carrier is Aetna, and Mercer serves as BOR. All communication is with the broker. I have exchanged previous e-mails requesting status as a viable bidder. The current 2012–13 premium stands at $6 million.

From: JGutschlag@GMSouthwest.com
To: BHamlin@Mer.com
Cc: LMcAdory@Mer.com

Subject: Bid for Brown U 2013–14
Date: 2-15-2013

Brian, good morning again. The experience you sent me lacks clarity in that the premium and claims are by calendar year versus school year. As an underwriter, I can't parse the claims' run-out from year to year. Can you provide experience by school year? Thanks,
JPG

From: BHamlin@Mer.com
Cc: LMcAdory@Mer.com
To: JGutschlag@GMSouthwest.com

Subject: Bid for Brown U 2013–14

Date: 2-17-2013

John, that's what we got from Aetna. I can request experience by school year from them. Before I do, please tell me why you will be a competitive bid versus all the others.
Regards,
Brian

⸺ꝯ⸺

From: JGutschlag@GMSouthwest.com
To: BHamlin@Mer.com
Cc: LMcAdory@Mer.com

Subject: Bid for Brown U 2013–14

Date: 2-18-2013

Brian, hey, begging your pardon, I didn't just fall off the hay wagon. As an underwriter and gauging my risk, I need experience by year paid claims: no IBNR and net premium, gross minus third-party fees and admin fees. Given that, I can determine profitability and see if there's any room for commission increase or multiyear premium guarantee.

⸺ꝯ⸺

From: BHam@hotmail.com
To: JGutschlag@GMSouthwest.com

Subject: Bid for Brown U 2013–14

Date: 2-18-2013

John, let me see what Aetna can do. I'll get back.
Regards,
Brian

From: BHam@hotmail.com
To: JGutschlag@GMSouthwest.com

Subject: Brown Bid Experience
Date: 2-21-2013

Attachment: BU Experience—net premium—paid claims 2009–10, 2010–11, 2011–12, 2012–13 partial.

John, this is confidential information, and please respond to my private e-mail. I don't want this coming back on me. Let me know what you can do!
Best Regards,
Brian

Note: I reviewed the sent experience and determined projected losses to be in the low sixtieth percentile, thus giving approximately 8–10 percent additional profit potential. So I sent the following e-mail.

To: BHam@hotmail.com
From: JGutschlag@GMSouthwest.com

Subject: BU 2013–14

Date: 2-26-2013

Brian, hey my man, now we're clicking. I can do you some good! First, I can lock the current premium rate for two years, with only a CPI increase for the third year. Students should love this. Secondly, I can increase your commission level 3 percent. At current premium, that equates to $180,000 per year. Lastly, we receive a 50 percent rebate from our provider network based upon our propriety discounts. As a potential partner, I'd share this with you 50/50. The estimate is $125,000.

Discount average = 40%
Savings = 25%
50% network rebate = 12.5%
50% Mercer share = 6.25%
Allowed claims (est.) = $5 million
Projected Mercer share = $125,000

All of this being palatable, I'll submit a bid based upon the terms above and look forward to being a Mercer/Brian partner @ Brown. Thanks!
JPG

From: BHam@hotmail.com
To: JGutschlag@GMSouthwest.com
Subject: BU 2013–14

Date: 3-1-2013

John, thanks! We'll see if we can make this work. From here on, respond to my company e-mail account.
Best Regards,
Brian

P.S. I like the Cowboys' new running-back trade.

Summary: The broker will sell himself out for commissions. He controls insurance-company reporting and fits it where it will best serve him. He will always say he's working on behalf of the student.

Bottom Line: Look at commissions and the resulting services rendered—do they match up? By the way, Mr. Brian, my potential partner, went with one of my competitors for more commissions! Students never participated in any of the profits, estimated at over $1 million per year, for this account.

CHAPTER 6

The Mouse That Roared

The Legal Process and What Happened

A criminal investigation can start with information being brought forth usually by a victim or person(s) associated with same who contacts a legal adviser, who in turn refers allegations to a district attorney or prosecutor. They determine if a grand jury needs to be involved to secure an indictment for prosecution. Subpoenas for documentation and persons knowledgeable about the case are sought to support the charges and subsequent appearance before the grand jury. After the determination of whether to indict, arraignment and a subsequent trial or plea bargaining follows and finally sentencing.

In my case, the victim, Virginia Tech University, located in Blacksburg, Virginia, had been an account of mine for more than twenty years. In 1994, the account came to me when I acquired the student book of business from BlueCross BlueShield of Virginia, later known as Trigon and, through acquisition, Anthem. The Blues had been in the student-health business for about five years, had mixed results in profitability, and was going public with a stock offering and thus wanted to clean up its product lines. The book was made up of thirty-five schools, but Tech was the largest and most prestigious. I bought the business for one times commissions (my fees for admin and profit) over three years. This equated to about 5 percent of collected premium per year, thus giving me about two-thirds net to cover my costs. I was comfortable we could do it for less than the Blues.

They had some personnel who sold and administered the business, and I wanted to hire some of the "hands-on" personnel. Jim Lane was an account rep and had a contact relationship with the schools and provider networks. These people are usually worth their weight.

I refer to Jim Lane as Jim Mousey, because it fits him better. He was no aristocrat. Lane was well educated, an MBA who understood finance. He was a purported family man and devoted husband.

You see, I never really knew this person. Initially, we had a small office in Roanoke, Virginia, with a couple of people doing administrative work, primarily for the Virginia Tech account. I never saw the office or even visited the campus. In earlier years, I had definitely made it a point to get to know all the accounts and visit them. As time passed, I had delegated that responsibility.

We converted to our premium system immediately and, over two years, weaned them off their claims system and onto ours. Years went by with Mousey actually running our office in Roanoke and continuing what I considered an excellent job of account management and renewal. My contact with Mousey became less frequent over the years. I saw him at the typical annual account-managers meeting at our offices and our Christmas party.

As I look back, I made a terrible mistake trusting Lane/Mousey to do the right thing. He had a certain con to his game. He brought a silver dollar for Tate when he was born. When we talked—and this was not often—he would always ask, "How's Tate doing?" I never met his wife or children.

Mousey set me up big-time. It was his idea to include the discounts with the paid claims in reporting. Trigon had reporting structured in that way. He assisted my IT director, Jim Caserotti, to develop the same type of reporting from our computer system. Mousey even told me that Fred Weaver, the risk manager from Virginia Tech, was OK with it. We didn't need to disclose proprietary discounts that Mousey had negotiated with the providers. Later, after my acquisition, Trigon actually got in legal trouble and paid fines for taking kickbacks on volume business directed to the providers. I have always wondered if Mousey had not done this same thing. He seemed to be a little flush with cash outside anything I paid him. Certainly, his scruples wouldn't have prevented it.

My organization kept me informed about our Virginia office as they deemed necessary. Mousey's shortfall: he wasn't a sales type and didn't present himself well, and so we couldn't grow our business. Thus, I brought in a new marketing director for national sales.

In 2010 there was a change of the guard when the Virginia Tech risk manager, Fred Weaver, retired. He had been there forever and, to my knowledge, was a close friend of Mousey's. They lunched and golfed together. The new person taking over, Ellen Douglas, had worked for Fred for nine years and was up to speed on the job description. Mousey, who was conservative but also a little negative, thought she might want to go out to bid because Tech hadn't in more than ten years. Usually, state schools are required to bid every three years just to be sure and to sample the marketplace. Mousey had the school at ease on this matter, but now there were smoke signals about bidding.

In later years, Mousey was lazy in any reporting to Virginia Tech. He didn't utilize our systems data and never accessed me as CEO. Simply put, his reporting was into the bogus category with no explanation. I didn't know what Mousey actually reported to Virginia Tech; I simply thought it was a "good ol' boy" relationship between himself and the risk manager. Mousey never even sent me a copy of any renewal correspondence, just an e-mail to my staff saying: "Tech renewed, no problem; buy a round on me."

Retrospectively, we reviewed the reporting Mousey gave Virginia Tech. He transposed experience from our system to Excel, including discounts until February 2006 of the 2005–06 school year. This was the year we brought subsidized graduate students into the program, and our insurance company underwriters were concerned about adverse selection due to older students, most with families. We had demanded a sizable premium-rate increase (38 percent), as the account hadn't been profitable for the previous two years. Mousey had indicated to Weaver my underwriting concerns. Weaver indicated back to Mousey that he thought he was being gouged and implied going for bid if this continued.

Well, as claims started to be realized for the 2005–06 year, it was obvious that the opposite was developing. The additional insured graduates were actually spreading the risk, and the additional premium charged was more than compensating for the increase in claims. The account was turning profitable! It was at this point that Mousey started to invent numbers that didn't look so good. He decreased the premium and increased the claims and *voilà*…a bad loss ratio.

Again, none of his Excel spreadsheet reports were from our system. He continued his masquerade of numbers, putting down what he thought the school personnel would believe. He was hooked.

Ellen Douglas started asking Mousey for premium reports. This was odd, because all premium was paid/collected through Tech's system and simply electronically transferred to ours via database conversion. Money was deposited locally in our Roanoke bank and swept overnight into our Dallas account. We had our system set up for checks and balances to account for the entire premium in the Tech system. The various insurance companies we utilized over many years always performed audits. Yet Ellen was making noise that her reports from Mousey didn't match the Tech system.

The dumb son of a bitch knew that Tech recorded every premium dollar paid by or on behalf of the students, and we simply duplicated it in our system. If you're suspicious of anything, it would start with premium reconciliation.

In early 2011, Mousey then began making statements to Carolyn Beck, my office manager, that he "didn't want to go to jail" for what Dallas was doing to reporting. At this point, Beck was asking me what to do, and school officials were calling me for the first time after Mousey had punted. I could see the quandary he had caused and figured the only way through it was to see if the discounts plus paid equaled Mousey's numbers. They didn't. However, the differences accumulated over four years were close. I thought it was best to go with it. Thus, it would tie back to our system.

Obviously, the school took the high road, saying had they known the actual figures, they might have gone out for bid or shopped for a lower premium rate. Our goose was cooked. They went out for bid, we were guilty of playing with numbers. The short of it: Mousey was fudging the premium and claim reports to make the loss ratio worse than what the system showed, thus making it easier for him to sell higher premium rates and make the school feel like they were getting a bargain or good deal. Mousey wasn't a good salesman and apparently felt this was the easy way to sell renewals.

Before this and behind the scenes, Mousey had gotten himself into a personal bind with his taxes. He had taken fraudulent business deductions while remodeling his home. The IRS was all over him and had him dead to rights. He went to his personal attorney and explained that he knew of a bigger fraud where he'd been a participant, receiving instructions from the top of the organization. His attorney plugged him in to the local district attorney's office, and Assistant United States attorney (AUSA) Tony Giorno surfaced. Giorno saw immediate stardom and reward to his career. He got permission from the attorney general's office in Washington, DC, to pursue a Racketeer Influenced and Corrupt Organizations Act (RICO) investigation, where all crimes point to the top without proof being required.

Giorno arranged for Mousey to enter the witness protection program as an informant to expose a criminal enterprise of great magnitude in exchange for leniency on his tax case. Mousey simply said that I, as the CEO, knew and orchestrated the bogus reports in order to charge higher rates and realize exorbitant profits for my company and the insurance carriers.

Mousey, under the direction of Giorno, immediately went to work, using his mole tactics to try to ensnare me, and my associates. He told Virginia Tech officials that Dallas had directed him on reporting and that the Dallas staff was directed by me. He solicited Carolyn Beck to generate reports matching experience reports he had already given the school. Beck never told me about this action, and this later became a charge of wire-transfer fraud. We also had a software program developed by our IT director that included a modifier to paid claims, so as to include incurred but not reported claims used for "incurred reporting." This modifier, input by the user, could not be accessed by anyone but Beck and other key officers of the company, for security purposes. Mousey knew this, and this was his approach to finger-pointing to the top. I never used this program.

Mousey got Fed permission to tape his phone conversations with me. Recordings made available later showed he tried to reach me four times, succeeding once on March 23, 2011, on my cell phone while I was driving. Although I was unaware of being taped, his call was peculiar because he kept directing questions to me like, "How did we produce the reports he had just received from our office?" Immediately, I knew something was up, because Mousey never asked for my input on reporting, and as a matter of fact, I didn't know what he had reported to Tech.

Mousy was just a little fish in a big ocean. There were other schools involved on a global basis. The Feds ate this up, especially since Virginia Tech, the victim, just four years earlier had experienced a disaster where thirty-two students were killed on campus—here we go again. The students had been wronged by inadequate security. This gave great incentive to the university officials to pursue this at all costs for the protection of their meal ticket: the students. Expanding the investigation could mean great media exposure, raises, bonuses, and promotions.

Mousey indicated to prosecutors that he was a puppet or on the receiving end of orders from the "don." By all outward appearances, I was orchestrating the false reporting. However, there was no proof in my e-mails, interoffice memos, or meeting transcripts that I was involved. But enter RICO, and that proof doesn't have to exist. Just being the go-to person at the top puts you in jeopardy. According to a statement by Mousey, I met with him and Beck on May 5, 2010, to determine how to falsify the reports. On that date, I was in Venice, Italy, enjoying my honeymoon, making love in a gondola.

Some time passed with advice coming to me to "let it grow hair," but in May 2012, the prosecutors summoned more than twenty-seven individuals to appear before the grand jury. I always thought of the grand jury as some unknown power in the sky, but in reality and in my case, it is a pawn use of the public sector—for the prosecutors to gain indictments of their choosing. Concerning insurance cases, the grand jury had little understanding, and what they did have was prejudiced; furthermore, this grand jury was held in Abingdon, Virginia, a small town in the Western Virginia boonies where the per capita income is $22,486.

Several of the persons summoned were former employees whom I had fired or who had had problems with my management style. Prosecutors badger, ask leading questions that are not permissible at trial, and get on record testimony that at trial is a slam dunk or an admission of perjury. My son and daughter, who were very much a part of the company, were put through hell as part of an in-your-face assault on me, their dad.

I had hired two legal firms to represent me. Both had attorneys who were former prosecutors who had grown tired of their Boy Scout ways and unfairness of the criminal prosecution system. The one-size-fits-all theory is not remotely fair, and neither is the attitude "the means justifies the end." Plus, there is more money to be made if you can pick your clients. I represented a pretty healthy prospect for them.

In June of 2012, we asked for a "reverse proffer", which has the Department of Justice (DOJ) present its case before any indictments are handed down. The problem: They don't have to fire all their cannons, and they can make allegations that can't be proven, just to scare the "person of interest."

The process was conducted by Giorno, local yokel prosecutors, and legal visitors from the attorney general's office in DC. They formatted a PowerPoint presentation with very little fact, a lot of fluff, and a conclusion of indictment for fifty-seven counts of mail and wire fraud under a RICO charge. *Wow, shit!*

I was blown away. My attorney took me into an adjoining room and said, "Think about it, John. You don't have to take it, but it would take your kids off the chopping block if you did."

My shock lasted several nanoseconds, and I said, "F——— the DOJ," and we left.

At this point, July 2012, things got more serious. I was served a civil suit by Virginia Tech asking for tens of millions in damages that also enjoined insurance companies that I had partnered the risk with for more than ten years. Tech's legal firm was also in Richmond, so mine and theirs endeavored to see if we couldn't work together. The insurance companies should have gotten together and sought me as a spokesman on their behalf, because they had set the premium rates that were charged to the students and were based on our actual system of premiums and claims. So the only wrong was they hadn't audited the reports sent to the school by Mousey, who by the way was an appointed agent to all of the insurance companies, and thus they were all culpable. The insurance company and I should have asked the right questions: "What was being reported to Tech or any account?" We should have established a system for reporting and renewal documentation, rather than relying on account reps to do their own thing. We could have settled for far less than each of four defending separately for more than $12 million.

As it was, I assisted Tech legal to get a more accurate picture of what happened and my minimal involvement in it. Mousey was the bad guy. October 25, 2012, I presented a *proffer* to the DOJ boys, where I laid out the case from my viewpoint, and my lawyers said it went well. On PowerPoint, I laid out the "dual set" theory, where the bid specifications from the school demanded a certain loss ratio be used, and the other side of this was the insurance company and what its profit model demanded. The only way to reconcile one to the other was to use IBNR reserves. Thus, I offered justification to serve two masters; otherwise, it was a catch-22. The DOJ boys who attended left scratching their heads. All said, the prosecutors had gone two and a half years, utilized government resources, had permission from DC for a RICO charge, and couldn't let go. Deliberate indifference became their mantra for guilty. This allowed the grand jury to proceed towards indictment.

Description	Assumptions
School Target Loss Ratio	82.0%
Completed experience Paid + IBNR	75%
Carrier Target Loss Ratio	70.0%
Carrier Underwriting rate increase	13%
Reporting Modifier for dual set	17%
Adjusted School Loss Ratio Paid + IBNR	88%
School Underwriting rate increase	13%

Figure 13. Dual-loss ratio: school and carrier

April 9, 2013, I was sitting on the porch of our suite at the Dell in San Diego with Brenda on our third wedding anniversary. We were having breakfast and enjoying the beautiful view of the property and the rolling surf. The naval base was nearby, and each morning at sunrise, the Navy SEALs went through their exercises and chanted their mantra. We couldn't hear what they were saying, but it was said in unison and made us proud as Americans to have these fine specimens of humankind on our side.

Figure 14. The Dell.

Suddenly the phone rang, and my lawyer informed me that I had been *indicted* for the same charges as in the government's reverse proffer, but with twenty years of jail time for each count—a sentence that Methuselah couldn't serve. Additionally horrific:They simultaneously froze all my assets, bank accounts, stocks, investments, real estate, autos...*all of it*! The same went for the operating company, GM-S, and its assets. Needless to say, our vacation came to an abrupt end, and we headed home. The news media had picked up the story, and AP and UPI distributed it nationwide. I received several calls expressing shock and sorrow, and my competitors smelled blood in the water.

When I returned to the office, I gathered our employees together and gave them the news from my viewpoint. They already knew quite a bit, as we had kept them in the loop of what was happening. I indicated that God does perform miracles; I definitely needed one. Basically, three things are needed for a miracle to even have a chance: (1) you have to be competent, know your subject matter, and believe in it; (2) it should benefit other people, particularly those less fortunate; and (3) you must have faith in God Almighty that it can happen but on his timetable. Many of my senior managers and several workers cried. I was so touched that they believed in me and that they didn't see me as the person so bleakly painted by the press.

In a quest to find some way to pay for my legal defense, I found a life insurance policy that was taken out in 1995 based on the wrongful death of my mother as a result of a legal settlement that yielded cash values available for a loan inside the policy. After a real struggle, the Feds agreed to let me use the loan value. This is a scary commentary about the DOJ and their wanting to be sure the deck is stacked to the hilt to ensure a win in court or to force a plea. This was difficult for me with limited funds for defense and a small-town anti-insurance jury.

We prepared for trial, and I had to provide a living-expense budget to the court for approval to gain partial relief of my assets. This allowed for a withdrawal each month that was audited by the court. The approval amount was about half our normal expenses. Remember, Brenda was a high-end spender, plus I supported my son, her elderly mother, and mentally disturbed son. Her side of the family was not about sacrificing and were use to someone else paying their way. I was cash short, big-time, as well as upset that I couldn't get cooperation from Brenda and her family. I discovered that the Feds had missed some cash values inside another life policy and my 401(k), which had been deposited with an employee-leasing payroll and benefit-service company. This was a third-party company and never hit the Feds' radar. It was risky, as technically I was in violation of the protective order. It was still upsetting to me that Brenda would not sacrifice at this time, simply because she felt I had the wherewithal to cover her expenses regardless. Thinking back, this ended up being several hundred thousand dollars that could have been used to bolster my defense. I was to be arraigned April 28, 2013, in Abingdon, Virginia, at 10:00 a.m. in Judge Jones's court 362.

My business partners and children, Kelly and John, traveled with me the night before. We flew from Dallas to Charlotte and rented a car, driving up through the Blue Ridge Mountains. The beautiful scenery helped take me away from the reality of our situation, if only for a moment. GM-S had also been indicted, and my children were the shareholders. We were to meet that evening with our lawyers, Bill Dinkin and John Davis, for discussion over dinner and some libation.

We discussed the lies, backstabbing, and lowball tactics used by the prosecutors to further their case. Bill and John both prosecutors turned defenders because of the DOJ's abuse of power and their desire to protect their indicted clients. I was high profile compared to most of their clients, who had committed documented, blatant criminal acts, and it was their attorneys' task to plea-bargain the best deal for them.

We discussed trial, witnesses, expert testimony, and refuting grand jury testimony. Our main problem was that I only had $175,000 in our legal fund: the cash values of my life insurance policy and $25,000 in personal funds from my daughter. We needed to get mileage on legal cost yet make the prosecutors work. John, a Harvard Law graduate and a bright guy, said he could attack the fifty-seven counts and felt he could get several counts tossed. Bill felt we could keep the prosecutor guessing and demonstrate that the trial was not going to be a slam dunk for the Feds.

The next morning in my hotel room and after showering, I heard the local news commentator on TV discussing a legal case set for arraignment today. Oh no! Surely this couldn't be mine! I hurried to look at the television. Sure enough, the commentator said, "A Texas company and its CEO will be arraigned for fraud and literally over-charging Virginia Tech students tens of millions of dollars for their health insurance." My heart sank—so this was how it was to be, guilty until proven innocent. This is the opposite of our constitutional rights.

As we arrived at the courthouse, one TV camera (probably all they had) and a couple of reporters were trying to rubberneck us and get close. It reminded me of so many TV programs I'd seen over the years. The rest of day was also reminiscent of television: standing before the judge, saying, "Yes, Your Honor," on strict instructions from my attorneys. I was taken downstairs by a deputy and fingerprinted and photographed while being watched by a cellful of Mexicans who looked every bit the role of druggies and dealers.

This was a big change, as from now on I would be part of the National Criminal Database that can be accessed by all law enforcement. I was definitely on their radar and would be looked at and treated differently from this day forth. I thought to myself at this low point, *Can I win at trial in this godforsaken hick town?*

The trial was looming. We had expert witnesses—good ones.

Mousey was a tainted witness, and the government knew it, but it didn't matter, as it's easy to point upstream and just say, "Doing what I was told." As my attorneys turned over the leaf on Mousey and questioned Virginia Johnson, the office manager in Roanoke, she said Mousey was like Jekyll and Hyde in that the church-going family man was into porn. His office computer was full of Google searches involving both soft- and hardcore porn. Mousey was indeed a man not to be trusted.

I had actually looked forward to a showdown at trial, because I knew Mousey and Beck would fold under intensive questioning. My attorney, John Davis, was capable of mean, in-your-face questioning. At the least there would be perjury charges against them.

I was really only concerned about the mentality of the jury being able to grasp the technical side of the reporting. Three days before trial and after extensive trial preparation, the prosecutors came with new charges that further expanded their case. This is known as "Ambush before trial: prosecutorial tactic to force plea bargaining." Here, the prosecutors are not required to divulge proof or evidence of these charges, only at trial. The defense lawyers naturally become paranoid and wonder if their client has kept pertinent information from them.

The prosecutors alleged that other schools outside of Virginia Tech were involved in bogus reporting, which put an enormous burden on our defense. The new charges indicated that eight other schools were involved but not specifically named and that I had knowledge of those specific schools. Also, Carolyn Beck, my Dallas office manager had entered the witness protection program and was prepared to testify. Also, my children were involved, stating from grand-jury testimony that actual paid claim experience was not used and instead a form of paid claims with a modifier. The government knew they had a tough case against me squared off with Mousey. There was no concrete proof of my directing Mousey on any of his misdeeds. They further indicated I had transferred "ill-gotten gains" to my children after the investigation was initiated (18 U.S.C. §Section 1957, Engage in Monetary Transactions in Property Derived from Specified Unlawful Activity). I knew that referred to the profit-sharing bonuses paid me by the carrier, which I equally shared with my children. This was all outside and apart from Mousey. This became burdensome to explain to a novice jury and added to my needed legal-defense funds. Also, there was a strong threat of additional indictments for both of my children.

This action preempted a timely (next-day) and crucial plea bargain deal presented by the prosecutors. They presented a fraction of the original 1,140 years(fifty-seven counts at twenty years each) jail time and $25 million in restitution. It was thirty months' jail time and $3 million in restitution. It became all or nothing, as to lose at trial would give me three squares a day in federal prison for the rest of my life but nothing for my dependents: a twelve-year-old son and a wife with no source of income, along with her mother and son who take in less than $1,200 a month in Social Security and Medicaid. In addition, Brenda was still giving me grief about her attending the trial. She made noise about being out of place in a small town and having to dress down. Her self-centered personality spoke volumes.

I took a final negotiated plea of eighteen months of prison time and $2.4 million in restitution to be joint and severally shared by the operating company GM-S. This seemed to be the best decision for *all*. Additionally, there was a contingency for Rule 35, which requires the prosecutors' recommendation for a reduced sentence based upon accepting responsibility and cooperation in the Virginia Tech civil case.

I had many meetings with Tech personnel and their lawyers, convincing them that the insurance companies who didn't want to work with me were culpable, as they had set the rates and didn't audit the reporting. They garnered major settlement dollars from the insurance companies. There were numerous other similar situations within the health industry, but the prosecutors were tired and wanted to move on.

My lawyers had the same attitude, and I was out of money.

Mousey received probation and $250,000 restitution requirement for his involvement with the Virginia Tech insurance fraud and his personal tax-fraud case. His creditability didn't matter, as the Feds would take their chances that a trial would not happen and Mousey wouldn't be called as a government witness. Beck also received probation.

I had to take responsibility for the crimes before the court. The CEO is where the buck stops. The Feds believed I had to have known and orchestrated this deception, that I was a Gambino Mafia chieftain pulling strings on my puppets, who actually were executing the crime. The sentencing judge would not accept my plea if I didn't take full responsibility, and I ran the risk of getting a much longer sentence. My lawyers stated over and over: "Be humble before the court and say, 'Yes, Your Honor.'"

At sentencing, the prosecutors were still saying I was not taking responsibility and tried to revert back to the thirty-month sentence. These guys would renege on any promise, because it's in their DNA. We had a good rebuttal on lack of evidence and paying substantial restitution. I got eighteen months and $2.4 million in restitution, which included $1.2 million being paid to Virginia Tech. That would be considered consumer relief, which would be tax deductible.

Supposedly, this was a good deal, with time to be served in a camp with other white-collar workers, judges, attorneys, and doctors—professional men who had fallen on the wrong side of the law. Camps were low security; I would be able to walk around campus in a relaxed environment.

Mousey and Beck were the ultimate test to a part of the Lord's Prayer: "Forgive those who trespass against you." I know I should even go one step further and offer them a blessing from the Lord. As of this writing, I am trying to get there.

The following are some grand jury testimonies that helped seal the indictments.

Grand Jury Testimony
Abingdon, Virginia
August 2012

Main Content: CEO directing traffic in the enterprise
Prosecutor: Jack Schitt
Witness: Jim Powell, former CFO of GM-S

Prosecutor: How would you describe CEO John P. Gutschlag?
Witness: Totally in command. When he said, "Jump," you would say, "How high?"
Prosecutor: Describe his controlling ways, please.

Witness:	One day he told me, "Hey, Powell, wire transfer fifty thousand dollars to my account. Today!"
Prosecutor:	Any reason given or what for?
Witness:	No, he said, "Just do it!" He was like the Holy Grail!
Prosecutor:	Mr. Powell, you are excused.
Witness:	Thank you, sir.
Background:	Jim Powell served as my CFO for two years. He was a CPA and came highly recommended by a headhunter, costing me $20,000 in placement fees. Mr. Powell screwed up my books on a one-for-one basis...with time worked equaling accounting entry errors. He would get totally confused on trying to record simple income and expenses. At one time, our books were $2 million out of balance. Transfers to my company account were based on funds still due from the original ESOP buyout of my stock and subject to our overall cash flow. I had to determine available cash as it was beyond the proficiency level of my CFO. It was booked as cost of sales (GM-S) and income to diversified (SID). I fired Powell for incompetence and spent many long hours unscrambling his accounting errors. Last heard, he was representing himself in prison ministry, where being right isn't required.
Summary:	The grand jury concluded that I was in control of my criminal enterprise, giving credence to a RICO charge.

Below I've included some more examples of grand jury testimonies: by an insurance company senior underwriter, my former in-house underwriter, and my national- marketing director.

Grand Jury Testimony
Abingdon, Virginia
August 2012

Subject: Client reporting
Prosecutor: Jack Schitt and Tony Giorno
Witness: John Nelson, ASR program manager/senior underwriter
Terminology: Loss ratio equals claims divided by premium

Prosecutor: You say IBNR can be added to client (school) reporting. What is IBNR?

Witness: Incurred but not reported future claim liability under the contract.

Prosecutor: Is it a set formula or figure to be added?

Witness: No, it is variable and can change by account.

Prosecutor: Oh, you can make it whatever?

Witness: No, it has to be specific but can change as future liability is realized.

Prosecutor: As I said, "make it whatever"?

Witness: No, there have to be specifics based upon historical run-out as a guide.

Prosecutor: So this insurance company can control its profitability?

Witness: Yes, to some extent.

Prosecutor: Well, let's get specific. If Tech had paid claims of three million dollars, say, through the end of the school year 2012–13, May 15, what would you report to the school in IBNR and paid claims?

Witness: Whatever the historical runout would be. Let's say if last year at the same time it was $1.8 million dollars [he computes it], it would be $5.4 million dollars.

Prosecutor:	What if you didn't have the account last year?
Witness:	We'd use industry standard.
Prosecutor:	OK, like LSU, which had a horrible loss ratio?
Witness:	Yes, they could be included.
Prosecutor:	So it certainly appears IBNR is totally controlled by the insurance company regardless if a profitable account deserves otherwise.
Witness:	We try to take all into account for fairness.
Prosecutor:	Fairness? You can add whatever you want. That's fairness?
Witness:	Well, it's not that simple.
Prosecutor:	[Turns to court reporter.] Read question two back for the record. You said it was variable and can change by account. IBNR appears to be like vapor; sometimes you can't see where you're going. Why can't you get your arms around this IBNR?
Witness:	We do and try to take everything into account.
Prosecutor:	Tech is an account that clearly ran a sixty percent loss ratio after the 2009–10 school year. Did you take that into account?
Witness:	Timing alone prevented us from retrospectively adjusting the rates.
Prosecutor:	It certainly appears you are talking out of both sides of your mouth and contradicting yourself. Mind what you've stated for the record; you can perjure yourself. Does IBNR as you've defined it here today represent fairness to the students at Virginia Tech?
Witness:	It probably needs further clarification.
Prosecutor:	Whose job is that?
Witness:	Well, we rely on SID (Student Insurance Diversified).

Prosecutor:	Who is in charge of SID?
Witness:	John P. Gutschlag.
Prosecutor:	Thank you, Mr. Nelson, you may step down.

Bottom Line: The grand jury had no understanding of IBNR being used on behalf of Virginia Tech students. Rather, they saw it as a deceptive means to garner excessive profits for the insurance company and its related parties. The upshot? I was in charge of a deceptive practice for the enterprise. The charge: RICO.

Grand Jury Testimony
Abingdon, Virginia
August 2012

Subject: Client reporting
Prosecutor: Jack Schitt
Witness: Clint Jackson, national marketing director

Prosecutor: Mr. Jackson, you stated that, in reporting to the schools, you included the discounts in the paid-claim figure. Why would you do that?

Witness: The discounts are proprietary and are not to be disclosed according to our contract with the provider.

Prosecutor: Mr. Jackson, if you had $100 claim and there was a $30 discount, how much is payable to the provider?

Witness: Seventy dollars.

Prosecutor: Good. How much do you report to the student who has the claim?

Witness: Well, this involves HIPPA, and it's confidential.

Prosecutor: Mr. Jackson, you're being cute and aren't answering this question.

Witness: I am not going to violate any confidentiality rules.

Prosecutor: So if this discount is added to the paid-claims figure, what does the report call that figure?

Witness: "Claims in full."

Prosecutor: What does that mean?

Witness: Claims including discounts.

Prosecutor: It doesn't say anything about discounts being included.

Witness: No, it's called "claims in full."

Prosecutor:	[Looks to the Grand Jury and turns to Jackson.] You're being deceptive and misleading. You're excused.
Witness:	OK, thank you, but I told the truth. I've got a plane to catch. [Laughing.] Can I get a police escort to the airport?

[Grand jury members snicker. Some laugh, and many shake their heads.]

Bottom Line:	Mr. Jackson came off as a hotdog deceptive sales guy who reported directly to the CEO, me.

Abingdon, Virginia
Grand Jury Testimony
September 2012

Subject:	Client reporting
Prosecutor:	Jack Schitt and Tony Giorno
Witness:	Clint Jackson, national marketing director

Prosecutor:	When you send a report on experience to a school, do you include claims that haven't yet been paid?
Witness:	Yes, this is called "incurred claims."
Prosecutor:	How can they be incurred if you don't know about them?
Witness:	It's based on historical occurrences with this account or with accounts that are similar in size.
Prosecutor:	Are you part of the team that puts these reports together? And if so, what's your role?

Witness: Yes, I help determine the modifier.

Prosecutor: Oh, so you modify the paid claims. Sounds like just jacking up the numbers. How do you determine the modifier?

Witness: It's a combination of completion factors, trend, benefit changes, and a couple more I can't think of now.

Prosecutor: Again, modifying to jack up claims so the school believes it's getting a great deal.

Witness: No! But hey, the government used a modifier for Obamacare to allow insurance companies an opportunity to adjust from their present loss ratios to the guideline of eighty percent.

Prosecutor: OK, let's get specific. With Virginia Tech, did you tell them you were using a modifier for their reports?

Witness: No, I didn't deal with Tech.

Prosecutor: Who did?

Witness: Jim Lane [Mousey] and whomever he worked with.

Prosecutor: Did Lane and his team tell Tech they were using a modifier?

Witness: Not to my knowledge.

Prosecutor: So the modifier is a way of disguising the real paid claims numbers and producing a smokescreen to competitors…so they can't bid?

Witness: Like I said, I didn't deal with Tech.

Prosecutor: You're the national-marketing director for all accounts. Jim Lane, by previous testimony, was your friend. He stayed at your house when in Dallas; you traveled and drank with him. But you didn't know he was modifying the claims for Tech?

Witness: No, sir.

Prosecutor:	What about your other accounts like American University? Reporting for them?
Witness:	I worked on American.
Prosecutor:	What was your modifier?
Witness:	Don't remember.
Prosecutor:	Well, do you just pluck it out of the air, or did you have a formula, or what?
Witness:	As I recall, it was a combination, as I stated earlier.
Prosecutor:	Did you get John Gutschlag's approval for this modifier?
Witness:	Oh yes, sir.
Prosecutor:	So he was the go-to or control person for the modifier?
Witness:	Yes, sir.
Prosecutor:	For the modifier, which serves to jack up the claims?
Witness:	I don't like the term "jack up."
Prosecutor:	Well, excuse me. [He turns to the grand jury.] "Change" to where the school or an outsider like a competitive insurance company can't see the actual paid claims?
Witness:	I just disagree with "jacking up."
Prosecutor:	Well, the proof is in the eye of the beholder, right, Mr. Jackson? [Looks at the grand jury.]
Witness:	They can have their opinion.
Prosecutor:	You're excused.

Bottom Line: The grand jury believed that "modifier" was just a fancy term for inflating claims experience. It also provided evidence of other schools being involved and a strong position for the government in filing additional charges. This added credence to claims fraud, wire fraud, and running a deceptive trade practice or criminal enterprise, meaning RICO and fifty-seven counts heading toward indictment.

Grand Jury Testimony
Abingdon, Virginia
October 2012

Major Content:	Years 2007– to 2011, regarding Virginia Tech
Prosecutor:	Jack Schitt
Witness:	Chris Christoplis, president of ASR, program management for Combined Insurance Co.

Prosecutor: If Tech's loss ratio finishes at sixty percent, why shouldn't you refund the difference between the final runout and the target seventy-five percent?

Witness: Timing prevents it. You don't necessarily know it will finish at sixty percent back when you're renewing the account for a new year.

Prosecutor: Refunds could be issued years later?

Witness: There was a change in carrier between years. The insurance company had locked in its profit.

Prosecutor: So a carrier is not going to share its exorbitant profits with the students?

Witness: It's a fully insured product, and there is no policy provision requiring the carrier to do so.

Prosecutor: I don't understand how you can take advantage of these students like this. Why can't you share?

Witness: In effect, we did, as we pooled the experience with LSU, and those students actually paid less than if underwritten individually.

Prosecutor: You're telling me you can tell a Virginia Tech parent that his student is paying part of the premium for an LSU student in—where?—Baton Rouge, Louisiana?

Witness: No, it's not that transparent.
Prosecutor: Why are you hiding things? It looks like deception to me.
Witness: No, it is an industry practice to pool experience.

Summary: You see the line of questioning. The grand jury came away with the summation that the program manager, myself, and the insurance company (carrier) were not forthright and were practicing deceptive trade tactics, leading to excessive profits that crossed state lines for wire fraud and money laundering—twenty-two counts out of the fifty-seven issued in the indictment. Oh, the Lord knows they don't understand.

Grand Jury Testimony
Abingdon, Virginia
October 2012

Subject: Client reporting, testimony on reporting to schools
Prosecutor: Jack Schitt
Witness: Karon Gidney, former underwriter and stockholder, GM-S

Prosecutor: How and what did you report to the client if experience was requested?

Witness: In various ways, depending upon the detail implied by their request.

Prosecutor: You mean, just anything goes or whatever you can get away with?

Witness: Yes, to some extent.

Prosecutor: Give me a specific example.

Witness: We had a software program that would add the discounts to the paid claims, thus grossing up the claims figure.

Prosecutor: So you misled the school on actual paid claims? Right?

Witness: No, not really. The report heading stated "claims," not "paid claims."

Prosecutor: Oh, so the client had to be able to interpret that?

Witness: I suppose. We knew the competition would receive a copy.

Prosecutor: Do you send a glossary of terms to the school on what you meant by report headlines?

Witness: No.

Prosecutor:	So you intentionally misled the school on its experience and the real status of its account and how it was performing?
Witness:	I guess. Even though we never intended any harm.
Prosecutor:	Did John Gutschlag know about this?
Witness:	Oh yes, sir!
Prosecutor:	Did he give you direction in doing so?
Witness:	Yes, sir.
Prosecutor:	You are excused, Ms. Gidney.
Witness:	Thank you, sir. I'll try to stay warm; it is sure cold here in Abingdon.

[Grand Jury laughs and smiles at Gidney.]

Bottom Line:
Karon Gidney put a nail in my coffin by not elaborating. Hey, payback for not paying her more for private company stock. The reporting method of adding discounts to paid claims was developed by Trigon BlueCross BlueShield of Virginia when they underwrote Virginia Tech's business. The reporting technique was acquired in buying the business. Insurance companies were aware of and approved of this method, as to explain it gave the competition an unearned advantage. The grand jury concluded that I was the mastermind behind fraudulent and misleading reporting, supporting wire fraud, money laundering, and RICO charges.

CHAPTER 7

Madoff Is Still in the House

FALSE REPORTING DISGUISES THE SUM of the parts equaling the whole. The massive fraud perpetrated in the student-health industry has left a trail of company and individual monetary enrichment. The fiduciary responsibility for the victims—namely, the students—exists only where it positively serves the insurance company, broker, or school official. In addition, the student victim group is naïve and lacks advocacy. Many brokers portray this as a service to the students and offer newsletters that discuss the basics of insurance, terminology, health aids, etc., but they always end up lining their pockets with the green in lieu of providing real saving principles to the students.

The $50-billion Madoff fraud, at its core, was all about fraudulent reporting. What the client received in reports didn't match the investment position. Madoff had an entire entity located on a separate floor of the high-rise building he owned, off limits, with hundreds of personnel to produce reports that were pure bogus. The banks and brokerage houses made no attempt to reconcile actual positions in the marketplace to the report issued to the client. Sounds too simple? Well, most people who receive an official-looking report (online or in the mail) regarding their financial statuses don't question whether it's worth the paper it's printed on. Madoff clients just leaned back in their easy chairs and said, "What a magician."

Madoff reporting, utilizing software modifications, based itself on compounding returns of 10 percent plus per year; thus, combined results of twenty-plus years were in excess of $50 billion.[7] The actual investment position was in the ballpark of $17 billion. Many investors didn't even lose their principals, just the inflated gains. The exposed Ponzi scheme provided an opening for lawyers, the Securities and Exchange Commission, and the DOJ to get more involved. After all, there was some *real* money to pay for fees and expenses.

Their combined results with a specially appointed legal task force recovered more than $12 billion of the principal, while they flittered away more than $1 billion for their legal fees and expenses. Madoff himself spent several billion on real estate, toys, and living the good life. The investors blamed Madoff for losing their investments when many recovered their initial principal. Many never connected to Madoff lost money in the markets over this time period. The Feds made sure the big boys—those with a billion plus in the Ponzi scheme—would take the major hit, trying to protect the little guy.

Madoff got 150 years in prison. His family took a real hit with suicide, early death, and overall disgrace. The computer programmers who set up the algorithms to compute the bogus figures got four years or less with meager restitution.

Madoff became a hero in prison. *The $50-billion-dollar man!*

Inmates would seek his sage advice for investments. He made many successful investments but spent most of the gains on his worldly pleasures. His losses were never recorded. His investment advice is still being communicated to inmate contacts on the outside to continue his savvy insight into the markets. Madoff actually enjoys the pressure-free environment of prison.

Although Madoff has been exposed for bogus reporting, the involved fiduciaries, banks, brokers and security companies have only plugged the hole in the dike. The structure of the dam or system hasn't been changed. The same modus operandi can happen again.

In the student industry, the hole hasn't even been plugged. It's still wide open to blatant fraud. Brokers, agents, third-party administrators, insurance companies, and school officials can act in concert or individually to overcharge students for their policies and, in one form or another, pocket the excess. Insurance companies can accomplish this by overstating incurred but not reported (IBNR) expenses and by directing their profits to future tax years or offsetting current-year losses in other product areas. Insurance company reserves are a powerful tool in controlling financial statements. Reserves play a major role in tax liability for current and subsequent years. Reserves and profits are inversely proportionate.

Madoff's reports are past tense, meaning they're supposed to record what has already happened, even if it was a fairy tale. Student reports are projecting what *may happen* in claims expenses two or three years down the road. It's hard to reconcile to the present, and the insurance company has every right to increase IBNR for future-year policyholder protection. Obamacare is attempting to track the reserves by policy year and, when the IBNR period is finally washed out, force refund payments based on the target loss ratios of 80–85 percent for individual/group policies respectively. However, the student school year splits two calendar years, and business can be straddled between two insurance companies owned by the same holding company—and I challenge any government actuary or accountant to figure that out.

Insurance companies are the most powerful financial institutions on the planet. They will always control their profitability by shuffling their reserves, and the government will be at least two football fields behind. Understand me: pinning all these parties down can be accomplished by specifically outlining the terminology used for experience reporting and by adopting a set of guidelines that must be utilized industrywide with an audit. Here are some examples of a few of these.

* **Collected premium:** total collected by the school, agent, insurance company, and TPA (all parties)
* **Net premium:** collected minus all third-party payments or that retained by the school

- **Gross versus net premium:** detail of third-party payments and retention
- **Paid claims:** actual paid to date, not including pending, denied, or IBNR
- **Incurred claims:** actual paid to date with IBNR
- **IBNR:** list components of what makes up IBNR (i.e., pending, completion factor, trend, change of benefits, etc.)
- **IBNR factor:** Actual claims *modifier* for the components of IBNR

Concerning reform, all experience reports should be signed by an officer or designated representative of the issuing insurance company, subject to audit. Violations of the guidelines are subject to premium adjustments of up to 80 percent of the misstatement, guaranteed for three years at the discretion and acceptance of the school. Individual participants will be reported to the respective department of insurance and/or the Consumer Affairs Commission for their respective disciplinary actions.

Following is an example of a claims report.

Claims Experience Report 2015/2016 as of 05/15/2016							
Account	Claims Received	Claims Allowed	Paid Claims	Discounts Allowed	Other Insurance	IBNR Factor	Total Incurred
USA College	$5,000	$4,500	$2,000	$1,300	$500	2.15%	$4,300

Figure 14. Claims experience report

Here are some notes to the above report.

1. If discounts were not a separate heading, then paid claims would equal $3,300 and incurred would equal $7,095.
2. The IBNR factor equals: (1) completion of claims 1.79, (2) trend 0.15, and (3) benefit changes 0.21, for a total of 2.15.

You start to see the complexity of reporting. Software can be flexible to provide a myriad of data combinations. The final result is undeniably tied to the system database, thus avoiding fraud, and by exacting terminology disclosure, deception is avoided. The burden of proof resides with the insurance company audit, checks, and balances.

The major banks and security firms involved with Madoff reporting have paid restitution and most of it in tax-deductible consumer relief payments. Audit is silent, but rest assured, some, but not all, client reports will be reviewed for authenticity. The student-health reporting is still open for change. *Currently, fraud and deception are prevalent.*

In the student-health industry, and in particular GM-S, reporting to the client was not structured. There were account representatives who had the primary responsibility to report experience to their clients. They had relationships with the schools and knew what to do regarding what was being asked for. My position was clear: "Don't give them any more than what they ask for, and then be general" (as almost every report given to the account ended up in the hands of the competitor). The schools felt obligated to share this information because of a greedy broker's advice, trying to make the service appear forthright but controlling the account or shopping for better premium rates or higher commissions in the marketplace. Some schools were loyal. Others would change vendors (insurance companies and administrators) for five cents per semester. I lost a bid at Nichols State by that amount. Louisiana State law dictated low bid prevails, regardless. Madoff clients receiving a pumped-up report showing fantastic results had no reason to change financial advisers. Likewise, with reverse psychology, an experience report to a school that showed poor results (a high claims-loss ratio) meant that school had no reason to change if it could get a no-change premium rate renewal.

I encouraged reports that centered on enrollment, type of service (CPTs), or diagnosis (ICDs)—anything but drilled-down premium and claims, which is what the underwriter needs to establish a profit model and issue a competitive premium rate. Now, when the reporting requirement was general yet contained specific "premium and claims experience," then I would advise using net premium (gross premium minus third-party expenses) and paid claims with pending claims and IBNR. Let's now look at detailed reporting and the problem it presents.

Say a school has one thousand students being charged a $2,000 annual premium per student. It's May 15 of the 2016 school year (final exams are over and the school is out for the summer). The school wants a renewal for the next year, 2016–17, commencing August 15. The experience report below is for the 2015–16 year through May 15, 2016.

Collected Premium (p)	**$2,000,000**
Paid Claims (c)	**$1,000,000**
Loss Ratio (c/p)	**50%**
Completion Factor (1)	**1.79**
Projected Claims	**$1,790,000**
Projected Loss Ratio	**89.5%**
Target Loss Ratio (2)	**75.0%**
Projected rate Increase	**20.0%**

Figure 15. Example of detailed renewal for the new school year

1. Completion factor = amount of claims incurred but not paid for the contract year
2. Reciprocal is expense and profit amount = 25 percent

The school will blow a gasket if its renewal rate is $2,400, or a $400 increase, when it only had a 50 percent loss ratio at the end of the school year. It will seek competitive bids, or it will be fodder for the controlling broker to move the business to another company, stating that the current company is using inflated IBNR. There is a myriad of these scenarios in the marketplace today. What can be believed, and who can a person rely on? School administrators are generally not adept insurance-wise, and so the situation lends itself to unscrupulous agents, brokers, marketing companies, and in some cases, insurance companies to take advantage.

Obviously, information technology (IT) can play an important role in reporting by adding IBNR factors to the paid claims. IBNR can include unexpected future claims such as these:

1. Change of benefits (like covering transgender expenses)
2. Change of trend (high-cost area beyond normal—e.g., NYC)
3. Time frame to pay claims (systems or software change)
4. Pending claims (meaning received but not processed to payment)

GM-S software was developed over time with input from more personnel outside the company than within it. The logic accumulated all the claims for a given school by benefit type. Certain benefits were not IBNR driven, like health-center charges and network-access fees, so the program has a matrix of acceptable benefit costs that allows the specific-account IBNR to serve as a modifier to the paid claims. Reporting would designate "incurred" in the heading of the report. Most schools had no clue what was meant by "incurred." However, competitive underwriters trying to develop a premium rate would pull their hair out because they couldn't determine the actual base number of paid claims to apply their own IBNR and generally would pass on issuing a quote. This tactic is also known as "controlling the marketplace."

Uniform, standardized terminology reporting should be an industry norm. Until then, everybody for him- or herself!

CHAPTER 8

Paying the Piper

LEARNING THE LIFE

I WALKED THROUGH THE FRONT door of a federal correction institution (FCI) on July 8, 2014. I was not under arrest, so I could report according to a marshal's written instructions: "Be there by noon or risk additional penalties."

This prison was in Fort Worth, Texas, forty-five minutes from my house. I was supposed to be sent to a camp, the least restrictive of prisons, but ended up at FCI, Fort Worth, because of my medical status: a pacemaker and other conditions that my attorney and I had stressed at sentencing, trying to secure home confinement, which backfired on us. This was a medical facility. I was put on medical hold, and any transfer to other facilities was negated.

Federal prisons are constructed according to the levels of security and types of inmates and their respective crimes. A supermaximum is designed to hold the most hardened and violent criminals. At the other end of the spectrum, a camp holds bad-boy doctors, lawyers, judges and other mostly white-collar crime guys. There are low and medium security prisons. My prison was constructed as a medium-security prison, with double twelve-foot chain-link fences with roll wire at the top and a lock-down concept, with five inmate counts per day. It was operated as a low security prison with the guards in control.

I was assigned to a ten-man room named the "Bus Stop," mainly be-cause it was where they dumped new inmates coming off the prison bus from a transfer station, usually Oklahoma City. The room was bunk bed–style, with individual lockers. It had a window air-conditioning unit—thank goodness, because it was a hundred degrees outside (July in Texas)! Cellies, or roommates, were from nineteen to seventy-eight years of age. I was the second oldest. Races? Black, Mexican, white, and shades thereof.

When I arrived, my fellow inmates were playing cards on a make-shift table. I went around to each of them, introduced myself, and shook their hands, just like I'd done many times at reinsurance or power-broker meetings. These new roommates looked at me like, "Who in the hell is this guy?"

I had to learn prison life. Understand, I'd never been in a jail cell or even a holding tank in my entire life. The prison compound was spread out, with housing facilities named for major cities in Texas: Austin, Dallas, Fort Worth, Houston, San Antonio, and Lubbock. The compound had clothing, recreation, commissary, dining, chapel, education, and medical facilities. Inmate count fluctuated between 1,800 and 2,100. The joke was that the food quantity stayed the same regardless of population, so any shortages had to be made up in com-missary, which was another profit center for the prison.

Over the first few days, various inmates would approach me and ask, "What are you in here for, Pops?"

My response was, "None of your damn business!" Well, little did I know how this system works. In medium- or higher-level prisons and according to law of the prisoners, every inmate has to show his paper, meaning his sentencing documents that clearly show what he's convict-ed for and the length of his sentence. This allows the inmates to classify each new arrival to a particular gang or place a price on his head (which says he'll have to pay for protection while incarcerated). These prisons are run by the various gang groups, and the guards stay out of the way to the point where their main duties are riot control and being absolutely sure that *nobody* gets out without proper paperwork. If an inmate escapes, it will result in major staff replacements or mass firings and negative career path changes.

Now, in a low prison, inmates are not required to show paper because it is not run by gangs, and the guards have a lot more control. In the BOP (Bureau of Prisons) system, inmates incarcerated in more secure prisons through good conduct can work their way to lower-security prisons. It's like a promotion. But if they foul up, chances are good, depending on severity of the infraction, that the inmates will be sent back to higher-security prisons.

So here I was telling the inmate scouts that I was not going to show paper. The report went back to one of the latent leaders of this action, and I was classified as a child molester or slime bag. When I learned of this, I immediately made my paper available to any and all. I almost wanted to post it on the bulletin board.

Circumstances then changed immediately. Inmates would approach me and ask me about RICO and what's it like to run a "criminal organization" or "enterprise." How did I pull this off, and how did the Feds catch me? After a short while of having a little fun with it, I basically wanted to be left alone. I was able to get inmates to run errands for me like laundry and commissary pickups. Many in passing would say, "How's Jon the Don?" Inmates are required to work, and the pay is nine to fifteen cents per hour. I never worked; I just had other inmates perform my work duties. I filled out the time sheets, and checks were deposited in my prison account. I paid them out of my commissary purchases and designated portions to the workers. Everyone was happy.

Finance plays a big role within the BOP. The annual prisoner reimbursement is approximately $33,000 for each inmate. This is government revenue funded by the taxpayers. The BOP is part of the DOJ, which oversees prosecution, punishment, and other counterparts such as the FBI (enforcement) and IRS (investigative).

Inmates were classified according to their health statuses, which is designated up front by the BOP in reviewing the health history and then certified or changed by the team of doctors or physician assistants (PA's) upon arrival for preliminary examination. There are four levels: (1) normal, no restrictions; (2) requiring regular health monitoring; (3) chronic, most with wheelchairs or walkers; and (4) confined and needing assistance.

A broad overview looks something like this for minimum income to FCI, Fort Worth:

1. 2,000 inmates at $33,000 per year = $66 million (taxpayer funded)
2. Commissary up to $325 month per inmate = $8 million (inmate funded)
3. Total = $74 million (minimum)

Medical level three warranted $57,000 income per year. I was level three, as were an estimated additional one thousand inmates. My unit (Dallas) housed four hundred inmates, more than half in wheelchairs/walkers. So total income was more than $100 million just for FCI, Fort Worth.

The interesting inmate maneuvering that exists at the beginning of a fiscal year (October) suggests this to be very lucrative for the BOP management. The annual reimbursement is up-front money, and as inmates are released or complete their sentences in the course of the year, only payments to halfway houses are reimbursed. This is a negotiated fee but is between $56 and $71 per diem. Take this understanding and extrapolate it for 215,000 inmates at 155 locations nationwide. This is big business and with profits and bonus potential, especially for the big cheeses.

The inmate cross section was amazing—not just in terms of race, but in education. Inmates who don't have high-school educations are required to earn a GED equivalency by the completion of their sentences. More than 50 percent could not read or write when entering prison. Most were Mexican or from Puerto Rico and could probably have gained accreditation in Spanish but no way in English.

The ages were from eighteen to ninety plus. The elderly were mainly sick, hobbled, and/or demented. It was pathetic to see the number of wheelchairs and the conditions of a large number of the men. They were nursing-home patients without nurses or caregivers to help them. However, in reality they got better care inside than they would have outside. Most had no families or had been disowned. They were without homes or incomes and didn't have insurance. This was a last stop for many and, in fairness, a better quality of life than on the outside, particularly those living under bridges.

Inmates died daily. We had 105 in one unit alone die in less than one year. The men had an assortment of ailments, mostly brought on by age, neglect, and lack of any moderate lifestyle. Diabetes was prevalent, due to obesity, poor diet, and complete lack of exercise. Many had been shot while performing their various crimes. (Yes, if they weren't killed, the government has the duty to take care of this group of ex-citizens.)

The shocker was the number of inmates who were gay and/or transgender. It was apparent that some had planned low-level criminal activities in order to be caught, sentenced, and imprisoned, where they could get hormone shots to expedite their female personas. It's quite an experience to stand at a urinal and have a transgender position him/herself at the urinal next to you. He/she has a good-size set of boobs and flops their penis out to pee. I never got used to that and couldn't relieve myself until *it* was gone.

Our country is arguing over whether public restrooms can be used in this matter or should be used according to one's birth certificate.

Well, in the federal prisons, they don't care—which overall is the attitude of the BOP. In fact, the BOP website has a section on statistics that is for public viewing or propaganda only and resembles little truth to the actual percentages on types of crime or gender.

More disturbing than this was the sheer number of child molesters. "Chomos" were estimated to be more than 40 percent of my prison's population. We termed them the "800 Club."

See, it goes something like this: Criminal prosecution for the past twenty years has been focused on drug trafficking, and incarceration numbers have mushroomed. Attorney General Eric Holder, because of political pressure for excessive sentencing and many cases where possession of small amounts of drugs would yield five to ten years, allowed a two-point reduction in sentencing guidelines for drug offenders. This meant six months to two years plus less time in prison. However, the emphasis for some time now has been on child pornography. The Internet has produced a proliferation of this activity. Websites and pictures are easy to access, and the Feds have set up numerous stings to entrap those who want to pursue sex with younger children sitting in front of their home computers. It's sick, but *this* prison was full of them. They make up their own stories—anything but the truth. In reality, technology is such that it's easy to track the computer users. The content cannot be erased, as hard-drive restoration can always find what was deleted. Also, the browser search content indicates user intent. Federal agents can show up at someone's door, demand a search, and find and haul away all the evidence needed to convict the user.

If the offender uploads child porn pictures, this is a more serious crime, as it's considered intent to distribute. If the accused arranges a meeting with an underage child, he can be convicted solely based on the travel to have sex. This keeps any victim from having to testify. The accused may not have had physical contact, but certainly his intent is known, and plea bargaining brings forward a variety of sentencing: five to twenty-five years. Trial is rarely an option, due to the embarrassment, media coverage, and difficulty of picking a nonbiased jury.

Now, from my position within this institution, most everyone around me was a chomo with varying degrees of involvement. The inmates do not want you to know details, and their papers are not readily available. So you may be talking, eating, and even bunking with some of the world's worst vermin. On the outside, I spent a lot of time (twenty plus years) contributing to, mentoring with, and being heavily involved in a charity run by Lutheran Social Services of the South (LSSS, now called Upbring) for sexually victimized children ages four to sixteen. Some hundred children or young adults were housed at the Nelson Center in Denton, Texas, trying to be rehabilitated to where a foster home was available to them within a two-year period. Some of the saddest stories I've ever witnessed poured forth when I was mentoring young victims or talking with staff members. I could see firsthand the horrors involved and the scar tissue left behind both mentally and physically on young innocent persons, usually by family members—Mom, Dad, or Uncle Ben. Now my imprisonment has forced me to deal with the inmates and their devil deeds to these young people. I've struggled with the second commandment of the New Testament, "Love they neighbor as thyself"; the Golden Rule; and trying to treat those inmates with some degree of respect, believing rehabilitation is possible for them as well.

A case in point: one month after my incarceration, a new inmate was placed in a bunk next to mine in the Bus Stop. Victor Duane Smith was a sixty-year-old black man who said he was from Hawaii, had worked with the Department of Energy, and had lost his family, wife, and two children to an experiment gone haywire in Los Alamos, New Mexico, apparently involving radiation. His retaliation against the federal government was to write software programs to steal funds from foreign bank accounts and deposit them in discreet remote entities for his future use. He said he and Edwin Snowden were described by Diane Sawyer as the two worst people on the planet.

This inmate sidled up to me and extended himself to me as a "butler" for chores (i.e., laundry, sheets, blankets, and commissary pickups). It was very helpful, as my arthritis was making it hard for me to walk any distances more than a couple hundred feet. He said he was also a physics graduate from MIT.

Now, I wasn't completely gullible, even though I'd been taken to the cleaners more than a few times. Anyway, I had my daughter, Tracy, check this man out on the Internet, only to find a stink bomb. This guy was into child pornography, viewing pictures in a public library. He'd had peon jobs and little education. The slime bag existed next to me in a federal prison that believes "one size fits all." I distanced myself from this individual, but suffice it to say, any blatant discrimination or physical harm on my part reported to the guards could result in time in the "hole" or additional time added to my sentence. Still, my position was to isolate myself from most everyone, not knowing who or what they represented.

CRIMINAL INFORMANTS AND COOPERATIVE WITNESSES

Criminal informants typically are intricately involved in the criminal process and inform the Feds or help them tape/gather information against target crime offenders. They agree to commit additional crimes to help snare the targets. Cooperative witnesses do the same, but they are intended to be witnesses at trial, meaning their covers will be blown, and so they are more vulnerable to retaliation from the targets.

In my case, I was the target "enterprise kingpin." Beck and Mousey were cooperative witnesses. I was told by my attorneys to refrain from any contact and certainly to never threaten them, either directly or indirectly. I knew the two, their strengths, but mostly their weaknesses. Mousey was lazy and not a good salesman, and he had memory problems due to a recent water-skiing accident. Beck had learned from me the way business is conducted—and not the wrong way. She wasn't real bright but worked hard to make up for her deficiencies.

I had hired John Davis—a tough Harvard Law graduate with a major law firm, William Mullins in Richmond—with the intent of drilling down these two at trial, as they would undoubtedly have to testify. I knew I could count on the fact that he could rip both cooperative witnesses to pieces, making them wish they had never agreed to enter the cooperative-witness program. I knew they were just trying to cover their own misdeeds and could probably get probated sentences in doing so. They had collaborated in producing false reports at Virginia Tech, and I knew at trial they couldn't connect me. At the very least, I knew they would perjure themselves at trial.

Interestingly, while incarcerated I learned there were several cooperative witnesses doing time. Their covers had been blown, damaging testimony had or would be produced in court, and retaliation was definitely possible. Therefore, the safe house is a low prison, which costs taxpayers a mere $33,000 a year. Even a Motel 6 with fast food and protection would easily triple this figure. The cooperative witnesses I met were very uneasy and were not trying to make new acquaintances. They were paranoid and, to some extent, were deprived of any peace of mind. At least a guilty plea and taking some responsibility results in a stress-lowering syndrome. They hadn't taken responsibility, only pointed fingers.

Beck and Mousey will forever know they had "self" stamped all over their foreheads, and implicating me will haunt them. If they've reached out to God for forgiveness—great! I have asked for forgiveness for both of them and their transgressions against me. I hope to meet them one day. I'm only looking for one statement: look me in the eyes and, without prodding, say, "I'm sorry!"

COMMANDING OFFICERS

In prison, a commanding officer (CO) can be a male or female staff member in charge of a housing unit for their shift, generally three per twenty-four-hour period. They are usually poorly educated, have not had training, make up rules that suit their characters. If they have a mean streak or manifesting anger, their guidelines can be very unfair.

Take, for example, Ralph, a fifty-five-year-old black man who usually worked the shift from midnight until 8:00 a.m. He was in charge of "a.m." counts—12:30, 2:30, and 4:30—and dismissal for morning chow. His was very crude and probably didn't have a grade-school education. He was regularly late on counts because of sleeping on the job.

At count time, all inmates are to be in their beds for an accurate accounting of the population, which is reported upstream all the way to DC. The BOP is insistent on knowing that all prisoners are accounted for at count. One night, I was in the restroom at 3:15 a.m., and Ralph was late for 2:30 a.m. count, he'd hollered at me, "Get back to your bunk, motherfucker!" He would be out of his head with barking orders.

At breakfast chow call, on Christmas morning, while we were being dismissed, one of the inmates said, "Merry Christmas, Ralph."

Ralph, with his unpleasant demeanor, responded, "The next inmate that gives me the Merry Christmas bullshit is going to the fucking hole." I had to look at this man and wonder, *Where's he going, and how in the world did he stay on the right side of the law?* Obviously he was not on God's.

Now, there are the exceptions. Salisberry, a twenty-five-year-old white CO, had a friendly smile, listened to us, and went about his job of unit control in a professional manner. How did this happen when there was no training school? Some people have good hearts, inspired by God's love, and their actions proclaim a pleasant and caring demeanor. I wish all guards had to be Christians, but in reality, this one-size-fits-all mentality makes for unfair rules because the general inmate population are a bunch of criminals who generally can't be trusted, would steal your underwear, and could backstab you in a heartbeat.

Yes, there are women commanding officers, and here is a breed who wants to exercise control. They regularly patrol the unit hallways, randomly searching lockers for contraband, and genuinely want to exhibit extreme women's rights, which to them means men are dog meat.

The biggest difficulty I had was the total lack of respect most COs had for the inmates. Most of them were the age of my grandchildren, and it was difficult to link my family to this bunch of scallywags, whose upbringing never taught them "respect earns respect" or "always consider your elders."

So the summary of all this is, CO control, even though unfair, is better than gang control, which is prevalent in the medium- and high-security facilities.

THE HOLE AND MEDICAL PROCEDURES

At seven one night, the CO told me to grab my meds, lock my locker, and follow him. He handed me off to a guard, who escorted me to the segregated housing unit, or SHU—better known to most as "the hole." He wouldn't tell me what for. My experience made me suspect Homeland Security guidelines and undoubtedly a medical procedure the next day that involved twelve-hour fasting. Homeland won't divulge timing of any outside movement for fear of inmate communication to outside confidants and a planned escape. Hey, it has happened. And the BOP does not trust inmates not to eat, so they throw them in the hole to guarantee it.

The hole is basically locked-down confinement and rigidly controlled. My cell in the hole, B05, housed one bunk bed, a steel toilet and washbasin, and a small, bolted-down table with an attached seat for one. I had a three-inch toothbrush and pack of toothpaste, along with a towel, sheets, and a blanket. Daylight was provided by a horizontal slit window four feet by six inches. The reinforced steel door had a vertical, eighteen-inch-by-five-inch glass window and a steel opening for food service or handcuffing, sixteen inches by five inches. When a guard approached, he unlocked this opening so he could cuff the inmate's arms behind him before entering. Guards took no chances in the hole. Most who were housed there were real hardened criminals who basically could not be mixed with the general population. These inmates hollered, yelled, cursed, and generally were like caged animals who were mad at the world. Not what you see in a zoo. One inmate, Frank Luciano, former Mafia lieutenant, led the pack in being sure no one slept.

Guard Vargas retrieved me at 7:00 a.m. after zero sleep. He cuffed me. This is the first time I'd been cuffed in my life. He was decent but wanted to show the other staff he had control of me. But it was one-on-one, with no cuffs, as he drove me to University of North Texas's health center. While there, in an exam waiting room, I noted five guards standing outside an exam room opposite mine. They were all wearing 9mm Glocks. I asked Vargas what the deal was, and he said they were his counterparts, except at Carswell, which is a medium-security women's prison also in Fort Worth. The lady was fifty-five or so and didn't appear to be a Clyde-type partner. Anyway, Vargas cuffed me for appearances, and the show went on. I sure wanted to know what crime(s) that woman had committed as she left, with guards surrounding her, hands close to their Glocks.

With her departure, my cuffs came off, and I completed my test. Then we embarked on a scenic drive around Fort Worth. We drove through some nice neighborhoods and the TCU campus. It appeared that Guard Vargas had an interest in the girls parading around in short shorts and skimpy halter tops. Actually, I hadn't been in the free world for more than thirteen months, and from my viewpoint, everything was exhilarating, bright, cheery, and enticing. Just a little bit of freedom, and I remembered what I had blocked out that day I'd stepped behind the walls.

Overall, it was a nice day, but the BOP's cost to monitor such medical excursion is of concern, particularly for the uniformed taxpayer. Prison personnel get time and a half for such trips. Estimated cost for just this excursion: $1,500. Who knows what the BOP paid for my procedure versus what a BlueCross BlueShield insurance company could negotiate. *One billion in medical costs is spent per year for federal prisoners.*

HEARING AIDS

I had entered into prison wearing hearing aids in both ears, indicated as such on my "medical duty status sheet" posted on my locker. I soon realized that getting replacement batteries would be a problem. The BOP doesn't keep an inventory and orders a minuscule supply. I had put my aids in an empty pill bottle after running out of batteries, and during a random locker search by one of the aggressive guards, they were discarded. At the time, I wasn't present. The guard, thinking contraband, didn't bother to check my medical duty status sheet, and I was left with the task of trying to file a claim to replace them. The BOP is cheap, believes inmates are liars, and typically doesn't take responsibility for its actions.

In this case, I was able to get acceptance from the regional BOP lawyer for employee negligence, with a stated settlement date of six months. I sent a written request asking what I should do in the meantime and received no response. I can't hear, and what I do hear is mostly garbage, so it did help me to isolate myself and stay out of trouble. But I couldn't hear counts or the PA system and had to rely on other inmates for, "Hey Gutschlag, heard your name, requiring you to report to…" My default? "Can't hear and didn't hear."

Another example of BOP negligence and deliberate indifference is that they have no one qualified in audiology, nor a plan in place to assist inmates with hearing deficiencies, estimated at 25 percent of the population. I even offered to pay for replacement out of my pocket ($6,000), and it had to be considered—for a six-month duration. In the meantime, I couldn't hear, was in isolation, and somewhat had peace of mind in spite of the inconsiderate BOP ("backward on purpose").

Six months after having my hearing aids tossed in the trash by Officer Willow, I was summoned to Lieutenant Christi's office. He proceeded to berate me for not supporting my claim form with receipts. He said "Why didn't you claim $10 million in losses"? I proceeded to tell him, "Because I don't lie and can produce proof of loss." I also mentioned that I had trouble hearing the commands for count and in the yard. Christi threatened me by saying "I'll put you the hole if you don't promptly respond to commands on the yard".

I was able to obtain receipts of the original purchase and, with the assistance of my daughter, Tracy, provide them to regional counsel, Mr. Sickel. In the report, I included the lieutenant's "hole" threat.

All in all, the BOP is trying to shirk its responsibility and, per its well-known strategy, hopes the inmate gets frustrated and throws in the towel. I have filed a complaint with the Office of the Inspector General in DC.

INMATE STORIES

Relying on Inmate.com to learn about prison can be very inaccurate and epitomizes poor factual communication. For a while, I sought to talk directly with some inmates and at least hear their own stories of why they were in prison and what they were going to change upon freedom. Would God be in their lives?

One inmate, Pops Curry, a former Hells Angel and Dirty Dozen biker, claimed to own land in Arkansas. He'd been married for thirty-eight years but would confuse his conversations between his wife and girlfriend. Pops discussed his many DWIs/DUIs in multiple states, talked freely about hijacking beer trucks and stealing slot machines from Indian reservations, and claimed to have beaucoup bucks, but nobody would send him money for commissary purchases. He begged me for a scoop of coffee. Sure, *no problemo*!

Inmates with child molestation offenses almost always have concocted stories for incarceration that keep their truths hidden. Curious inmates simply memorize those inmates' IDs (provided on all uniforms issued) and contact people on the outside, who can then look up the ID numbers on the BOP website and discover their real stories. Usually, it is vastly different from what they tell on the inside.

An inmate across from me, Campfire Fred, was serving twenty-five years for molesting young boy scouts while acting as an influential leader of the Boy Scouts of America organization. His last offense was molesting a three-year-old little girl. While incarcerated, he was caught cutting out pictures of little boys, drawing penises on them, and building a scrapbook. Other stories are too morbid and disgusting to repeat.

One inmate, Kevin Sanders, a convicted child molester, had reached a blatant place in his life and his rationale, as he related it to me on the compound one afternoon was as follows: "Today, young teenage girls and many even younger are more advanced sexually than the law permits. The courts can try a teenager for murder but not hold her responsible for soliciting sex. Sex slavery is big in this country and entraps innocent men looking for a good time. I'm attracted to smooth, unwrinkled skin. Also, I should be able to look at nude pictures of young girls based on the Freedom of Information Act. Our media and YouTube will allow anyone to look at a beheading performed by ISIS. Why not child pictures?"

The general feeling by inmates not involved with chomo activities is: punish them in severe ways, but be careful not to bring about reprisals. The chomos themselves actually enjoy a carefree atmosphere in prison, in that guards and staff protect them from discrimination, and disciplinary action will be taken against those who threaten this awful breed. I always asked them, "Have you changed your life since being incarcerated?" without discussing their offenses. I believe that God will forgive them if they genuinely ask him in humble prayer. But they have to change and can't slip back into old, horrible habits. If I get the inference of God-given change, I want to talk with them; otherwise, I distance myself big-time. If you get in the face of a rebellious chomo, he'll say, "Let's go see the CO," and guess what? You'll be going to the hole for unfair discrimination.

Another inmate, Scott Perchamp, used his shrimp boat to haul marijuana and cocaine from Mexico and the Dominican Republic to Florida and Texas for delivery. He made millions, but he always had patterns, routes, and the same drops, which were detectable, making it only a matter of time until he was brought down. Scott got fifteen years and lost most all of his assets, but ballooned up to four hundred pounds while laying around eating honeybuns in prison.

Nacho Fernandez was a drug hauler between Dallas and Los Angeles. He and his eighteen-wheeler rig could make $20,000 for a thirty-six-hour round trip being part of a drug ring. His associations, in the roundup of this small cartel, went down in a domino-like fashion and got him fifteen years.

Brett Welch, age fifty-six, came in the same day as I did. Brett ran a head shop in Wichita for twenty years. He knew the paraphernalia being sold was used for drugs but took the position that it was buyers' problem, and he was not in charge of their lives. Brett sold K2 for five years, when it was not an illegal drug. Periodically, he would check with an administrative assistant at the Drug Enforcement Agency in Kansas

City to see if the legal status had changed. Once it had, he continued to sell the drug illegally. The Feds observed him for months. His spending habits had increased. It was easy for the Feds to access an informant CI to orchestrate illegal purchases.

One evening the Feds acted. Helicopters, squad cars, and a SWAT team descended on his house and took all his possessions, including his wife's jewelry and son's guitar. Brett only received fourteen months but was literally broke, and his family, who depended upon him, was without.

Because we came in together, I felt somewhat as a fatherly figure to him. He was so sad and couldn't adjust to incarceration. He was a chain smoker, and while the BOP manual said they had a smoking-cessation program, they actually did not. Doctors wouldn't give him his pain meds or the drugs given by his outside docs. He was a mess and would regularly choke up about the situation he had left his family in. I invited him to our nightly prayer meetings and reprimanded him for using the "GD" curse word. It was not because of me or what I did to help him, but one day I saw that Brett was going to make it. Now he could see daylight (he had three months left) and said he had more appreciation for his wife and business principles.

Life has to change from what it was when inmates arrived; otherwise, they're destined to failure. One's future is proportionate to the changes one makes and your positive relationship with God.

MORE INMATE STORIES

During my time in prison, I discovered that some of the inmates had interesting and somewhat humorous stories. Keep in mind, though, that the truth could only be verified via the Internet and then usually not to that level of detail.

In a room across from mine, one inmate, Jimmy McQuire, an eighty-year-old mortician and funeral-home owner/director. He sold burial policies—gold, silver, and bronze—for $6,000, $3,000, and $1,500 respectively, which he self-insured. The problem? Jimmy took the premium payments to Vegas, believing he could win big; still pay the burial costs; and have a surplus left over for his enjoyment. He liked the women, too.

Good fortune isn't always in the cards in Vegas, and Jimmy finally lost it all and had to face an ugly fraud case. Jimmy, sad to say, lost his wife while incarcerated, and the warden wouldn't let him go to the funeral. It was probably just as well, as some mighty unhappy hometown folks, particularly the younger set, might have been inclined to take things into their own hands. Jimmy was planning on sticking around FCI for some time, and the prison does have burial plots for the indigent.

Infestations of scabies permeate the housing units. Some inmates don't shower regularly, and wheelchairs, catheters, urinary bottles, asbestos, and mold make for an unhealthy environment. A lot of four-, six-, and eight-man rooms were fumigated and the inmates sent to the hole to be isolated from the others. BOP medical officers don't try to culture or verify the actual diseases or their origination.

On New Year's Eve, a guard caught an inmate under a blanket talking to his girlfriend on a cell phone while extremely drunk. Sooo many questions, but obvious answers. The cell phones are sold for around $1,500. Booze is inmate-made, with corn, rice, wheat, and sugar. What is not available in the mess hall or commissary is offered by the guards. Most guards are undereducated and slow on the intelligence meter and like the power part of the job, telling men (doctors, lawyers) old enough to be their fathers what to do and how, and making up rules as they go. Salaries for guards are typically $40,000 to $50,000, and they try to earn extra income by smuggling contraband—and it happens every day.

I had several leather products made by the prison leather shop for my family members. Actually Christmas presents for 2014. I shipped the products out in daily mail—outgoing mail is not checked by the guards—and made arrangements for my son to write checks to a contact person on the outside that benefited the producing inmates family. Everyone was happy.

The internal monetary system of exchange is as follows: mailer, first class postage, $0.49; mackerel, $1.15; honeybun, $1.05; or any other combination of three hundred commissary items. Gambling bets are based on full books of stamps (twenty times $0.49 equals $9.80). I bet ten books (roughly $100) on a Cowboys game and got the spread out of the library newspaper delivered daily. Sports gambling is big inside.

Inmate Fred Cellini—age seventy, imprisoned for more than twenty-five years with no end in sight—knew how to label other inmates. Fred himself was an interesting story. A lawyer by trade, on the outside he had organized a holding company and bought distressed small-town banks. He found an easy way to tap federal funds. If his group put up $20 million of bank rescue capital, the Feds would match it ten to one. So with more than $200 million of new capital, he could move and shake on loans, money laundering with his Mafia connections. A not-so-bright woman serving as a messenger to send cash offshore left a briefcase of cash in a limo by mistake, and the FBI traced the prints back to the woman, who implicated Fred and others.

Fred, doing beaucoup years for bank and wire fraud as well as money laundering, was one savvy prisoner. Curiosity about other inmates killed the cat. I would say, "Fred, guy standing over in the corner."

Fred would size him up and reply, "Drug dealer."

Again, I would say, "Fred, guy standing by the north wall."

He would say, "Chomo."

It was fascinating. How did he know these labels where inmates didn't have to show their papers? Of course, Fred, being a big-name lawyer on the outside, would take on inmate cases for divorce, sentencing issues, etc., and would note the crimes on their papers. But his time in multiple prisons gave him the insight.

Inmates would somewhat label themselves by who they hung with. Old white guys with no tattoos, looking like Grandpa Ned, were most often chomos. You could envision them searching the web, downloading child porn, or hanging out on chat sites with fifteen-year-olds who appeared to be there just to please but turned out to be FBI agents in disguise…oops!

The drug dealers were rough, tough-looking guys with tattoos head to toe—not sure about all parts, but never wanted to know or see. Very few blacks were chomos; rather, they were there for drugs or aggregated assault.

Drug dealers who made millions selling now claim they were ahead of their time regarding new laws and legal access to marijuana in many states. They forget or won't recall how they sold without prejudice to children, the already hooked, and/or anybody who had the money. And they would do it again because of their selfish nature, regardless of the law. Mexicans were almost 100 percent drugs, mainly young kids playing delivery boy and getting five years. They were grossly undereducated, and few spoke English. Prison was like a country club to them, with three square meals, a bed, and no bills or child support to pay.

The cross section of inmates was amazing: at least 40 percent chomos, 30 percent drugs, and the remainder were financial, bank robbery, murder, or government witness protection program. "One size fits all" is a real injustice to the system and the inmates who serve time.

Another inmate, Shipp Crawford, was a hard-core drug-smuggler pilot who had flown thousands of kilos of marijuana and cocaine before being nabbed by the DEA tracking flights from Mexico to McAllen. He kept up with the population mix and had been in the system for twenty-five years at twelve locations. He said FCI, Fort Worth, was the worst prison for chomos getting the easy life and everyone else getting crappy food and medical care.

I just tried to stay out of trouble and do my time, get closer to God, and figure a way via the criminal law code to go home. I spent a lot of time in the law library. There was a complete computerized version of the criminal code available on second-generation desktop computers. I focused mainly on Title 18 U.S.C. §Sections 3621, 3624, and 7310.04. This all dealt with conditions for early release due to compassionate issues or being eligible for home confinement. I qualified because of my age, the nonserious nature of my offense, having a dependent child, my pacemaker, other health concerns, and outside income to support me. Everything appeared positive. I wrote letters to the regional counsel, visited my case manager, and literally bugged anyone in a staff position I figured could help. At sentencing, we had pushed for home confinement, only to get short-circuited to this dump. Home confinement was my daily hope. It kept me full of faith and focused on a positive ruling.

After about six months of almost daily scouring of the criminal code, writing letters, and you name it, I realized that the whole appeals process was strictly for the public or media benefit. The sheer ability to appeal your plight and the elaborate details of how to file and accomplish the same was nothing but a hoax. The Nazi minister of propaganda, Joseph Goebbels, must have written the script.

My only hope for early release was the 15 percent reduction each year for time served, based on good conduct. This meant my eighteen-month sentence was reduced to 15.3 months, if I was a good boy. The only good thing about this charade of potential home confinement was that it gave me energy, focus, and hope for about half my time in prison. After this, it was kind of downhill, because I could see daylight. Most inmates couldn't see a flicker of light.

SATURDAY NIGHT IN A FEDERAL PRISON

The place is like a zoo. As you go from one living space to another, you witness different behavior and adaptations to the living environment.

Overall, all inmates have standard-issue clothing that includes five complete sets of shirts, trousers, T-shirts, socks, and boxers. I believe that is where common ground ends. First, there is no personal appearance code other than no gaudy necklaces, earrings, or piercings. Most inmates shave their heads, get prison buzz cuts, or never get haircuts. Some hair is midback, ponytailed, or with the blacks, dreadlocks in knitted hair bags, some sticking out two to three feet. There are beards of all shapes (Santa Claus, hippie-type), most not groomed in any way, where if they were on the outside, you would definitely distance yourself or cross the street to avoid walking past them. Inside, the inmates are on their best behavior; one slipup, and they're put in the hole or shipped out to a higher-security compound. However, their "best" is whatever they can get away with.

The Mexican Mafia is a close-knit group. They stick together and speak pretty much zero English. This helped me, because I really didn't want to know their conversation and couldn't pick out the cuss words. They are a party group, talking nonstop (gibberish to me), laughing and actually celebrating that prison life is far better than the outside free world, only with less money.

The black guerilla family (BGF) also grouped up in their cells and especially at chow. Their conversations—if you can call it that—were laced with cuss words. A typical sentence might be, "The motherfucker told me, 'Fuck off,' and I told the motherfucker, 'Fuck you.'" Literally a nonexistent vocabulary, with zero grammar. How in the world could they gain employment or meaningful jobs, careers, or anything rewarding to them or their families?

The whites have some segregation; many are Aryan Nation. One such inmate, Jay Ward (a drug dealer and proud of it), had tattoos over much of his body with the names of five of his children, all with separate mothers, tattooed around his neck. He readily admitted he hadn't seen them in years or at all and bragged about not paying child support.

A lot of the whites might be termed "trailer trash," and most prided themselves on knowing how to beat the system by being able to go to chow early with counterfeit or expired diabetes cards, not checked by the guards. Their stealing of food from the mess hall by food-service personnel was unparalleled. They would sneak out with thirty to forty-five pounds of meat and vegetables strapped to their bodies or stuffed into their clothes—more with winter jackets on. They ate it, sold it, and/or made booze from it.

These distinct groups do not mix well and exist on their own. Where there are gangs in higher-level prisons, in FCI, Fort Worth, they stick together as gangs, just without the enforcement. In all social groups smoking and drinking is prevalent, but usually in bathrooms with ventilators and inmate lookouts.

RELIGION IN THE COMPOUND

FCI, Fort Worth, has religious ceremonies in Spanish and English for Protestants, Catholics, Muslims, Hindus, Jehovah's Witnesses, Mormons, and a couple others that I have no clue about. I can really only speak to English Protestant, as that's my background, having been awarded ten years of perfect attendance at Sunday school at an early age. Later, I served as an elder, usher, and financial chairman for a large Lutheran church. I had a good Christian foundation, thanks to my parents, who saw to it. My attendance and teaching was Christian.

I fell away from the church later in my life, when I always spent Sundays at my ostrich ranch. Those were days based on work and cleaning up; fitting church service in was not practical. We had our pastor come to the ranch periodically for communion and Christian fellowship. However, I felt that God had given me some tools to work with and expected me to practice in his name by way of his scripture to produce a bountiful yield returned to others and to him.

Then I went through the two and a half years of DOJ investigation. While enduring the harassment of the federal prosecutors, I tried to counter with prayer power, both individually and with a group, to keep my strength and focus. I realized I was losing the battle and that my Christian leadership needed to be retooled.

I attended Protestant service at the FCI on that first Sunday and kept that commitment going forward. I reopened myself to God, realizing I needed to change and that I couldn't leave that place with the same religious understanding I'd had when incarcerated. I needed a closer relationship with the Lord. The following is how I tried to direct myself:

- Have faith that the Lord knows my future and has a plan for me that will be revealed within his time frame.
- Develop a better communication with the Lord through prayer that praises him and so that my actions please him.
- Understand the true meaning of "forgive our sins and those who sin against us." I am not to judge those who don't forgive me.
- Try to develop a better practice to love thy neighbor as thyself.

In prison, my experience was that there were very few Christians. There were those who proclaimed it but didn't practice it, taking the name of the Lord in vain as regular practice without the least bit of hesitation.

Most inmates have broken families and were raised in dire conditions. They either don't know their mothers and fathers or have resentment toward them. Many inmates have killed and would do it again. The teardrop tattoo indicates they have, or it's seen as a status symbol if they haven't.

Stealing is prevalent everywhere. During my time there, I had my underwear, purchased for a premium at commissary, stolen from my laundry loop and shoes stolen off my cell floor during INT (institutional nap time). The amount of food stolen from food service is a big business of resale to inmates. My favorite dish, meatloaf, can be had for, say, two mailers (ninety-eight cents).

Thievery is everywhere, and you can trust no one. Here is an axiom I heard several times: "Adultery and coveting are not sins if the woman is consensual or you need something you don't have." Holy mother of Jesus…what is wrong?

I attended nightly prayer meetings. At first, I was happy to meet inmates who shared my enthusiasm for group prayer. As time passed and I became more in tune as to who were the chomos, I realized there were several in our prayer group. I ended up taking the position that I was not a judge, even though I abhorred their crime. After all, they may have been reaching out to the Lord in prayer to ask forgiveness and for change. One individual, Mandy, was seen being close to a transgender inmate, and that made it difficult for me to shake his hand as we concluded our prayer meetings.

I struggled with my association with known child violators, and I decided that I wanted to continue work on the outside to assist their victims. Solutions regarding these perpetrators is kind of like birth control: don't have children. Their crimes are harder to follow up on, particularly when Child Protective Services gets involved. If we provide education, it only sidesteps the issue. Most child molesters have been molested themselves. We need to break the vicious circle.

Indictments and prison time don't cure their morbid desires. We are filling out prisons at a greater rate than we did with drug offenders fifteen to twenty years ago. In both instances, the offender often goes back to his previous bad habits when released. Shame becomes an ingredient for change. I wanted to explore this on the outside with my reconnection to Upbring (formerly LSSS) and the charity work I'd done in the past regarding the victims. Publicized shame, prisons segregated to this type of crime, and religion to change one's lifestyle is a combination that appears to have a shot.

LIFE FROM THE BOP SIDE

If I were in charge of the BOP, here's how I would it: I would completely separate child pornography or molestation. This group should not be allowed to mix with the general population and ideally would have their own prisons.

Guards should be largely ex-military and have in-depth training for consistency of enforcing set rules and grounds for punishment. Their training would include sensitivity and practice for mutual respect. A statistical database on guard offenses would be used for reviews, promotions, and terminations, and also tabulation of inmate filings and harassment considered.

Education needs to be revamped for licensing in the trades and office administration, with a heavy weight placed on technology. English and language skills would be made a priority. GEDs have little impact on future job placement.

Under my leadership, the guidelines for good conduct time (GCT) credits would be revamped to include double current or one-hundred-days-per-year reduction in time to be served. In conjunction, penalties would be harsh and electronically posted for offenses on the compound, these by degree of severity: Intentionally being physical to another inmate or staff member, fifty days; crashing lines for pills or chow, five days; contraband, twenty days; and making booze or drugs, thirty to a hundred days. Technology would allow guards to post penalties of minor status instantaneously online, with printed status distributed in mail call. Keep in mind *online* doesn't mean the Internet but rather the prisons' central databases. Penalties over fifty would be signed off by counselors and a unit manager.

Technology would play a larger role, with thumbprint verification for pill-line prescription pickup and chow. Here's an example for the pill line: Upon entry to the pharmacy area, the inmates' thumb scans trigger an overhead display screen showing the first five who scanned. If the first inmate in the order doesn't appear in thirty seconds, that inmate drops to second. Second miss drops to five on the list, and then to the default list for penalty. Others move up the electronic list in progression of sign in.

Remember, prison is for convicted criminals who have proven to be disruptive to society in one way or another. Disagreements with the BOP system should involve an appeal process, which currently is a farce. Basically, 8K–11K (unit, warden, region, and DC) is just a way to allow appeal but never grant any form of leniency or fairness. I would appoint a committee of ten inmates elected by those staff guards who deal with the inmates on a daily basis. This group would meet two to three times a week (they have nothing else to do), screen the bogus appeals, and recommend those that have merit. Unit managers, counselors, and case managers would sign off or, in some cases, route to the warden or region. Bad boys need to be locked up, and it's no picnic or travel venture. Finding those wanting real change in their lives is the challenge.

German prisons see a high level of success by giving inmates comfortable cells, complete with personal decorations and flowers. The main issue is to earn respect you have to show respect, be it staff or inmate.

THE NONSOCIALITE

After being incarcerated for almost a year, I found myself withdrawn from even trying to communicate with other inmates. I had no intention of reaching out or connecting with ex-cons. Also, it was against my probation requirements. The horrible guise of placing all crimes together makes for characters from a Steven King novel. You can't get your hands around just who they are or what they stand for. You sit next to an inmate in the chow hall who raped and murdered his twelve-year-old niece and now participates in your nightly prayer group. Later, you witness his conversation latent with cuss words, taking the name of the Lord in vain and with contempt for others. A lot of really bad guys are in a low-modeled prison for their own protection, as a higher-security prison, run by gangs, assures their physical harm or death.

The second commandment of the New Testament ("Love thy neighbor as thyself") becomes very difficult to practice. Are these people real? They're not honest with themselves and live in a make-believe world. Worse, communication with them is a farce. In fact, 45 percent of federal inmates have mental problems. How can you love your neighbor when you can't reach anything spiritual? The worldly physical side is pathetic!

I've noticed that the longer you are incarcerated, the less chance you have for meaningful reentry into society. I was surrounded by nonstop cursing, hateful resentment of our government, and general denial of any wrongdoing. Many inmates had lost track with the outside free world. I wanted out of this nightmarish place. Finding those wanting real change in their lives...that is the challenge!

I was released on September 8, 2015, only to be sent to a halfway house in Hutchins, Texas, operated by Volunteers of America (VOA). Supposedly, this was just a stop before going home to serve the remainder of my sentence under home confinement. Just some paperwork, I was told. But as in typical BOP style, truth is fleeting.

The VOA program, while getting compensated by the BOP for $60 to $70 per diem per person, provided indoctrination to the free world and series of classes to ready former inmates for proper reentry to society. The classes were a complete joke and just another waste of taxpayer money. The process of completing the classes was geared for two weeks—obviously tied to some bean counter's business plan. Also, the object of reentry was to find a job. So the wannabe-free guys had to go out during the day (or while not taking classes) and interview for jobs. I was exempt because of age and medical reasons. My roomies would look in the phone-book yellow pages and jot down any companies on their work sheets to be submitted to the front desk for departure times. Vans would leave in the morning, taking the would-be employees to the bus station nearby so they could navigate around Dallas via the transit system to find gainful employment. What really happened was their girlfriends or, in some cases, wives would pick them up at the station and they'd party, screw, sell drugs, or whatever. One of my roomies had a wad of cash on him that would choke a horse. Keep in mind, this group of reentry inmates is considered the cream of the crop. The real bad boys stay home at the penitentiary.

Anyway, I completed my classes in two weeks and was released for home confinement. This program allowed certain freedom away from the designated house. In this case, my daughter Kelly's home had passed probation-officer inspection. I had to fill out a schedule as to where I was going when I left the house. I had to have a landline, as they would randomly call me to be sure I was home when I was not scheduled to be away. What they didn't tell me was that additionally they could call me at random and insist on a trip back to their facility for drug testing. In my case, in sentencing, drugs or alcohol were not even listed as a need to test—better stated, no testing was required. I didn't have their permit to drive yet, so I had to have a family member cart me forty-five miles through downtown Dallas and return up to three times per week. Additionally, the random calls for at-home presence would come at 3:00 a.m. or 4:00 a.m., and if I didn't answer after two attempts, the VOA would call the sheriff to come get me.

This indicates that there must have been many previous violations to the home confinement program. The DOJ is a broken program in dire need of revamping, and much evidence given to the one-size-fits-all program is *outdated* by the types of crimes now being committed and certainly doesn't address gender or education issues.

I was formally released from the BOP on October 28, 2015. I voted in the November elections less than one week later. This is one benefit I had as an American that they didn't compromise. It felt good to vote for my choice of candidate without some strong arm overseeing me.

Sooo glad to be free and an American!

CHAPTER 9

My Last...
(Continued from chapter 4)

BEFORE THE VIRGINIA TECH INVESTIGATION, I had started to build a new house for Brenda and me. Additionally, I needed to take on care for her mother and disabled son. She agreed to be a mom to Tate, as his real mother was still trying to climb out of the bottle of booze and pills. Brenda was a beautiful woman, nine years younger than I, but she was high maintenance and in need of a fat checkbook that never got low on checks. She was raised in an evangelist family, with both mother and father as preachers. Brenda was very musically talented and tried to make it on the outside, but the timing for her style of music and a lack of good connections and leadership kept her from making any real money. She enjoyed the good life: loved to travel, eat at fancy restaurants, and go places to be seen. She often told me, "Let's have fun while we can. Your kids can run the business, and you can hire Derek [her other son, who was very bright] to run the business with them."

The DOJ investigation of Jim Lane (Mousey started in early 2011 after he was charged by the IRS for falsifying his returns. Mousey turned government witness in February 2011. Prior to that time, I was enjoying my marriage, building a house, traveling, and buying things with and for Brenda. As they say, when the cat's away, the mice will play. Mousey and other account managers used this unchecked freedom to bogus up reports to make renewals more attractive to the schools.

The indictments of GM-S and myself stated that I ran a criminal enterprise and directed personnel under my control to engage in criminal activities, such as mail and wire fraud and victimizing students. My forty-four-year tenure in the student-health market made me the kingpin to running the criminal enterprise and fit a RICO charge, much as the Colombo, Gambino, and Genovese families pulled strings from afar without getting physically involved in the actual crimes. The company and I suffered irreparable harm to our reputations and business opportunities. Suffice it to say, the government personnel—be it the IRS, prosecutors, FBI, or judges—all bent their rules, manipulated the grand jury, and lied when they thought the case was turning south on them. They ruined a twenty-eight-year-old company that brought innovative products to the marketplace and saved students out-of-pocket costs far exceeding prosecutor or victim claims for damages. Nevertheless, I had to take responsibility for what had happened…ugh…*muy difícil.*

Life with Brenda under the same roof, with her mother and her fouled-up son living in my old house next door, was not Disneyland. Brenda had a set pattern of maintenance appointments starting at noon or after, followed by a late lunch or combo dinner and more appointments, only to arrive home late. She would ask me to join her and was irritated if I had a reason not to. My life involved getting up in the morning at 5:30 a.m., getting Tate (nine years old) breakfast and off to school, reading the morning news, working out, and heading to the office at 9:00 a.m. At this time, the Fed investigation was heating up. I had hired a defense lawyer, grand-jury subpoenas were being issued, and I was trying to keep the business going. Still, I left to pick up Tate from school at 4:00 p.m.; I felt committed to him, as his innocence and security was paramount to me. Brenda felt and said that I loved him more than her.

Sometimes I would find a sitter or take Tate with me, and the three of us would eat out together. This never happened at home unless someone stopped for fast food and we ate watching TV. We never had a sit-down cooked meal, the three of us, with prayer. Many times Brenda would come home after Tate and I had gone to bed. She would stay up watching old movies, some that were pretty risqué. She fancied herself a diva or movie star entertainer who had just missed the big time, strictly by the hand of fate. When we did go out, we argued repeatedly, with the central theme being what I had or had not done. I hadn't bought her a sweater on our honeymoon, hadn't shown affection to her while displaying ourselves to the travel group (Tauck Intl.), hadn't helped unpack from the move, resented her mother and son, and everything else that happens between dawn and night.

We were really two ships passing in the night. I had so much going on at the office; she had really no clue about business and was not a good listener. She would counter with, "Let the kids run things" or "Hire Derek." What kind of business was I running to let a "numb nut" like Mousey issue fraudulent reports without my knowing it? She couldn't see the forest for the trees. Several bottles of wine (and Brenda didn't have high capacity for alcohol), and we were off to the arguing races—many times with Tate present.

And Brenda could spend with the best of them. She would literally shop every day. Each morning, her two-hour get-it-together produced a striking woman. She could walk into a high-end store, and immediately the sales clerk or, better, the owner would know they had a live one. They would compliment her on her beauty and what she was wearing and suggest the latest sale in the store, whether a dress, accessories, or a pair of shoes. She could walk the talk, fill up her Escalade, and lose the sales receipts. At times, I would ask, "Hey, baby, what did you buy for fifteen hundred dollars at Niemen's this week?"

She would counter, "I don't like your tone of voice," and then set up her argument around the fact that I hadn't bought it for her. She would point out that I should realize that nice things are for those you love. "Don't you love me?" she would ask.

Overall, she was a walking, talking shopping addict. She didn't care if there was money in the account or if I was under federal indictment with an asset-protection order from April 8, 2013, to final sentencing on May 21, 2014.

We argued, and on a couple of occasions, things got physical. One night, we were heading home from SĒR restaurant and arguing over whether her son looking at porn would have an influence on Tate. She said, "Boys will be boys, and you can't keep them from it." Voices were raised, I called her a bitch, and she hit me in the face. I called her a fucking bitch, and she clobbered me. I probably had it coming, but she was more talented at fighting than I realized. My nose and eyes were a bloody mess. At home, I took several selfie pics for later evidence, if need be.

On another occasion, the argument ended up in Tate's bedroom. This was the day after my pacemaker was surgically implanted. She had had several glasses of wine (we typically drank two bottles, which usually meant I had five glasses and she had three plus a cordial). She brushed quickly by me, striking my pacemaker shoulder, and I pushed her in return. With her six-inch heels snagging the shag carpet, she went down, striking her head on the wall and putting a hole in it. This event has been played before more people, lawyers, and cops than a B-rated movie. She called 911. Later, she voluntarily went to the ER, with her mother driving. There was no medical record of trauma or injury and no police report of domestic violence, and it was never even suggested that I be charged, go to jail, or leave the house. I did ask her for forgiveness, but I witnessed that Brenda had never learned the counterpart "forgive those who trespass against us." For a religious person, I never understood this, but this is her issue with the Lord, and I've had to let it go.

We had spent sixty years apart in life and were very different people, and she filed for divorce while I was in prison, claiming domestic violence and all of my assets. I said to myself, *While in this darkness of my own, I need peace, and this woman doesn't know how to give it. God has a plan for me, and it probably doesn't include her or her family.* I've learned to try to interrupt God's way. Amen to the future.

The whole divorce thing got more complicated when I was released from federal prison to a halfway house on September 8, 2015. At this point, we were under a settled mediation agreement that gave her $10,000 per month for her expenses and a 44 percent split on the net proceeds on the sale of the house that was built for *us*. This was a great departure from a claim to all of my assets. She couldn't prove domestic violence and didn't have claim to community property, as most of my assets were earned before we were married (this was a big reason for no prenup). Also, she had been caught many times in her own lies, and her attorney was growing weary of the striking women who had walked into his office on Turtle Creek (high rent area) claiming cruelty and physical beating from a convicted felon who was going to serve time for RICO.

She had actually signed a contract with attorney Joe Amberson on June 11, 2014, around the same time as we drove to view from a distance where I was to be incarcerated. I remember her sitting in my car looking at a hell hole and telling me, "Honey, it will be all right; you've got my love and support." Later, in that same prison, where I went to the library to read the daily newspaper, do legal research, and basically pass the time in a not-too-bad environment, I opened up a large unabridged dictionary and looked up the definition of *bitch*. The first definition was "a female dog." The second was "a spiteful woman." Wow, did this fit. I would have never been in trouble with my mouth and Brenda, if

I'd simply said, "Bren, you're being a little spiteful today, honey." And…
did she fornicate? Yes, if the conditions and money were right.

All we had to do was sell the fricking house, which I had more than
$1.1 million invested in. In mediation, My lawyer (I was still incarcer-
ated) won a major issue of what to list the house for. If it didn't sell in
thirty days, we would drop the selling price 10 percent until it sold. At
this point, Brenda proved to be stubborn and at the first stage of mental
instability. She wouldn't answer the phone for a sales agent trying to
schedule an appointment to show the house. She refused to allow a lock-
box on the door, and if a sales agent was finally able to get in touch with
her, she would indicate that her mother was ill and the house couldn't
be shown.

(I'll back up a little. When she filed for divorce on me while I was
in prison, my attorney had her mother and son evicted from my other
house, only to walk seventy-five feet to a million-dollar-plus home that
had sixty-nine hundred square feet to house three people. I never felt
sorry about this, as it became clear her mother had taught Brenda well
on the principle of using OPM.)

If someone actually made it as far as a showing, she would tell them
the Internet speeds were slow in the area, the water was disgustingly
bad, etc. She did not want to give up on *her* house, regardless of what
the court order said.

Despite all this, we received a contract on the house for $775,000
on August 11, 2015, with closing and occupancy in thirty days. She did
zero planning for a move, and the week before the scheduled closing,
she demanded $50,000 in order to move. I knew this was a stalling ploy,
as she had hopes of being able to remediate the divorce and thought I
couldn't fund the move. I came with the $50,000 in three days. She
went to plan *B*…or *F*—I'm not sure where her mind was at this point—
which was to claim that the chandeliers were hers, and she should be
able to take them with her. I had paid more than $20,000, and there

were nine of them, some very beautiful if you're into displaying materialism. The new buyers also loved them, and their attorney threatened lawsuit, expenses for delay, and mental anguish. This drove the price down even more, just to be able to close the sale.

At this point, it got wild. She hired a company to take the chandeliers down and had her mentally incompetent son, Jonathan, and his live-in girlfriend haul them away. He was arrested on a public highway on a charge of domestic violence (beating the crap out of his girlfriend) with the chandeliers in the car. The car was in my name, and the Frisco police came to my house (actually daughter Kelly's') to see if I knew about what was going on with Jonathan and the girl (Esmeralda). Needless to say, they had already checked police records, noting that I was a convicted felon just recently released from a federal penitentiary. Yes, I had a twitch, but I knew they were just tracking facts. Almost simultaneously, Brenda filed a stolen-objects report with the Denton police, claiming the chandeliers at a $50,000 value. Jonathan went to jail on a domestic-violence charge. Esmeralda returned the chandeliers to the front porch of the house...or to be more accurate, dumped them damaged on the porch. Brenda claimed to the police that she had found the stolen items and had them returned. (The police were just happy to exit this situation.)

Brenda claimed through her attorney that she was the heroine and just trying to cooperate. We had a court date to address the contempt charge, which was why she didn't move when the court ordered her to. At the hearing, the judge was very upset that Brenda hadn't done what the court ordered and wanted to know why. Brenda asked to approach the bench (her attorney had dismissed himself from the case), and the judge ordered her to speak from her position. Brenda stated she had filed for bankruptcy in a Houston court. The judge was infuriated but stated that we couldn't go forward with this hearing until the bankruptcy issue was resolved.

Brenda filed a totally bogus petition with the bankruptcy court in Houston, stating among other mistruths that she had lived in Houston for the past six months and was working for $1,600 per month as a domestic assistant for WingSpread LLC, which is owned by...guess who?

At this point, Mr. Kevin Samuel Price surfaced from his lair. Their whole scheme, filed in writing to the court, was to claim the house as her only asset, as she was penniless because of her wealthy husband's desire to drag her through the travesties of life. She claimed her debtors to be only my children, whom she and Kevin knew wouldn't have proof of anything owed. Therefore, under Chapter 13 of the bankruptcy code, the house could be awarded to her minus any debt. There was none. She went to this level to get a house to be hers that she never paid one cent for and which I had already proven was not community property. Yet she was enough in love with this piece of concrete, brick, mortar, and wood to go to these lengths.

One other comedy point here. She claimed in the petition to be a former Miss Kentucky (she was not) and even sent the judge her picture. Yes, believe me, this person named Brenda Carol Golden believes men are basically stupid and that a large set of boobs will persuade them to make decisions that are not always rational or correct. Why do you suppose I'm saying this?

My attorney traveled to Houston for the bankruptcy hearing. Brenda represented herself and got completely smoked by my attorney and the judge. The case was dismissed, and the judge ordered her to not file in any other jurisdiction in the entire United States. Brenda told my attorney afterward with startled eyes, "I am completely defeated."

Brenda had agreed to sign the property deed, but not on her split of the proceeds. Closing took place on November 30, 2015, but our funds were held in escrow until we could come together with the judge on what were her expenses regarding her misconduct and purposeful delays. We had subpoenaed her bank records in the meantime. I knew she had a separate account, but until the divorce filing, I never suspected clandestine activity. The bank statements showed cash deposits by you know who since March of 2014. There may have been some prior to this, as we only asked for eighteen months of records. Kevin Price had been a lifeline to her. She cherished material security, and I guess when she felt I was not the cash cow she thought she had married, she returned to Mr. Generosity. There was nothing this woman wouldn't do for her self-preservation. It was getting scary, and I wanted *out*!

We returned to court in front of an angry Judge Barnes at 367 District Court in Denton, Texas. The judge asked my attorney if he sought jail time for her contempt charges, and with my permission, he said *no*. A yes would have meant at least thirty days, and it might have been a good thing for Brenda to eat some humble pie, but benevolence overruled.

Brenda got less than $160,000 after being ordered to pay more than $70,000 in legal fees. She had stood to pocket more than $400,000 if she had just adhered to the mediation agreement. In what she finally received, her 44 percent equated to a gross selling price of $427,000. This was a million-dollar home. She also received more than $200,000 in jewelry and other household furnishings. Her materialism displayed itself brightly. Try to turn these items into food or life necessities, and you'll get ten to fifteen cents on the dollar. Brenda went for the whole enchilada and got the sauce.

She now faces IRS scrutiny, as when she filed for bankruptcy, they found she hadn't filed returns for the past four years. Upon further investigation, it came out that she hadn't filed in more than eighteen years, as Kevin Price gave her cash to live on or as a salesperson. No income was traceable. Kevin had told me not to include her in my returns, as it would raise a flag with the tax boys. I figured he should know.

Now, I wonder if an IRS agent is looking at her bank statements. You could clearly conclude that cash was being deposited by Price. Was he taking a deduction for it on his return, or more importantly, was Brenda declaring the deposits as income? If not, it appears to be tax avoidance. Ouch! That will result in penalty, interest, and *time*. Also, she claimed a portion of Tate's social security benefit, stating she was his custodian when I was incarcerated, when in fact, my older son, John, gallantly performed those duties. The Social Security Administration will have to sort this mess out, but suffice it to say, I'm doing no risk talking with any government agency.

All said, I'm humbly gracious for how this ended. We were not meant for each other and need to move on to God's *next* plan for both of us.

I know eternal life has no place for resentment or disdain. Forgiveness is the only answer in being able to move to God's next step. Brenda has many talents and burdens. I tried, but I wasn't the man to complement or resolve them. I hope to meet her again in the hereafter and witness that she has done well with her life after me.

FINAL REFLECTION

I never recall praying for a woman who would take care of herself. I do recall somewhat resenting my first wife for not doing so, and I did wish that I could find a woman who did. Be careful for what you wish and/or pray for; be specific, as the results may not be to your liking. This turns out to not be risk taking but rather *gambling*, where you have no control of the outcome.

At this point in my life (July 2016), an awful lot of foul water has gone under the old bridge. I don't see another marriage in my life, but a woman companion is still desirable. One I could mutually communicate with and love, and who would just be my best friend. It's difficult for Tate, as like it or not, he has seen more negative with my relationships than he should have, being a young boy growing up with me. Most of the time, it's been just him and me. I will respect that going forward. I do pray for a meaningful relationship in the future that includes both Tate and me. But it's not in the cards unless it's God's way.

Epilogue

ACCEPTING RESPONSIBILITY FOR MY ACTIONS was a must at sentencing to avoid a worst-case scenario. After my prison experience, I certainly don't want to retrace my path; however, the government's willingness to cheat, lie, and set a person up for conviction at all costs is extremely unfair and can lead to innocent persons being convicted. All said, I accept the fact that I knew of false reporting in my office and did nothing about it. I followed the adage that everyone else was doing it in the industry, and I wasn't on a mission to curtail it. Rather, I chose to lead the good life. Now I have adjusted my lifestyle and feel closer to God and family, and I know in my heart that it is dead flat wrong to mislead less knowledgeable people in order to gain financially.

It's been over nine months since my release from federal prison. Here is an update.

My case of the missing hearing aids has been ruled by the Office of the Inspector General in favor of the DOJ, as the guard accused of trashing the aids has testified that he didn't do so, and the inmate who indicated the same is trying to profit at the expense of the government. There you go...the same as a dictator of a third-world country. They are always right, regardless of fact...no exceptions!

My taxes were a mess, mainly because my wife had tossed many of my records while I was incarcerated, so I had to re-create most. The issue on tax deductibility of restitution payments made for consumer relief became muddled. Bank of America had taken a $7 billion deduction on the same issue of consumer relief in dealing with the housing debacle of 2008–11; however, my tax attorneys were not able to assure me that the IRS wouldn't audit me, reject the deduction, and charge me penalties and interest, or even expand its investigative processes. I wanted nothing to do with any government entity investigation going forward. It's difficult to come out on top if the other side can interpret the situation to its liking and/or bend the rules. The DOJ proved it has that power, and I wouldn't *risk* that the IRS wouldn't do the same.

Kimi, my second wife, has resurfaced in glorious fashion. She's been clean for more than twenty-six months, has remarried, has a solid paralegal job, and has been reintroduced to Tate as his missing mother. Their relationship is solid; she has every other weekend with him and takes him to dinner on Tuesdays. Tate still smiles when he sees her but doesn't have that stare of "when will she return?" The three of us couldn't be happier and more relieved.

I've sold the two homes that I had in Aubrey. I bought a beautiful, smaller home in McKinney, Texas, that Tate and I enjoy. He has made many friends and looks forward to his eighth-grade year as a fourteen-year-old. He says he's not ready for the drama associated with girls...yet. Also, for me drama is a synonym for risk.

Insurance departments in several states have contacted me for assistance in cleaning up the student-health industry and its shortfalls. However far this goes is uncertain, as there are many examples of students and schools getting exceptional premium pricing to the point where no victims can be found.

Don Vito Corleone does not exist in the industry, but Madoff reporting techniques make it still open to deceptive criminal activity, false reporting, and monopolistic control. Standardized reporting with uniform guidelines/definitions, and penalties/fees charged for noncompliance, is the easy solution to this sham. This could be part of a national student-health association or an independent rating service, but definitely not a federal government–run entity.

I've reconnected with Upbring, but it seems their willingness to explore the child molester side is weak at best. Their resources are all about finding foster homes for abused children, not trying to educate/rehabilitate the numbers of molesters or stem the vicious circle of a victim likely to become an offender.

My struggle with the second commandment has reconciled itself to this: "See yourself as God sees you. Accept yourself as God accepts you. And finally, accept others as God has accepted you."

I've seen Brenda from afar, sitting at the bar in Perry's new steakhouse in Frisco, showing her girlfriends pictures of the house I built and that we tried to live in. She has leased and lives with her mother in a three-thousand-square-foot house nearby. Jonathan was sentenced to two years in the state penitentiary for domestic violence and illegal drug use.

God is good. I'm much more spiritual and completely open to his guidance, as he knows my skills better than I do. *I'm waiting for orders from headquarters.*

RICO (Racketeer Influenced and Corrupt Organizations) Act

Formerly Racketeering Investigation of a Criminal Organization (1970)

THE FEDERAL GOVERNMENT ACCUSED ME of running a criminal enterprise whose objective was "enriching, promoting, and protecting" my influence and power over hundreds, if not thousands, of insurance/reinsurance companies and their agents and brokers. The group or individuals were part of the criminal organization or enterprise.

A RICO violation is an overreaction charge created by the federal government to allow it to prosecute organized-crime bosses who successfully insulate themselves from the everyday activities of their crime families. Under this statute, a prosecutor doesn't have to prove that the head of this criminal enterprise even knew that crimes are being committed—just that people under his or her leadership or employment committed two or more predicate acts. Under this theory, the head of any organization is responsible for the actions of every employee. RICO is an easy jury-trial conviction. Reasonable doubt does not have to be proven to the jury. You could throw it against the wall with all the other charges, and some of them or just RICO would stick, resulting in a *twenty-year sentence*!

The federal government has never lost a RICO case at trial.

GM Partnerships

THE GM BRAND HAS A history of many partners over the course of my business career. Early on, while organizing Affiliated Computer Systems Inc. to go public, I had partners Jack Murphy, who was president of Keystone Life Insurance Company, and Billy McKenzie, who served as my mentor in the computer-software business. Later, Ellison Miles was a board member and partner in oil/gas production. We drilled several wells in partnership. Bob McBride was an early partner in the ranch ownership. Mary Ann Maher was an employee and later partner in the student-insurance business. "G" always signified Gutschlag, whereas "M" was a variable.

Cardinal Rules, Awareness, and Guidelines for a CEO

1. Insulate yourself from the client. Personal friendships and business do not coexist.
2. Client-reporting responsibilities are designated outside your office. Establish audit and punishment for violation.
3. If you are in the twilight years of your career, resign as CEO and take the title of chairman emeritus—as defined in the bylaws, not responsible for employee or third-party misdeeds, deception, or fraud that may lead to criminal prosecution.
4. Subordinates capitalize on the lack of specifics.
5. It is lonely at the top. In a fire, everyone runs for his or her own cover.
6. Auditing, delegation, and cross-checking are the best allies.
7. Remember, your boss is God, and you *do* report and answer to him.

Made in the USA
Columbia, SC
26 July 2018